Tom Baird

DESIGN
and
TECHNOLOGY
in
ACTION

COMMUNICATING DESIGN

HEINEMANN
EDUCATIONAL

About the series

Design and Technology in Action is a stimulating resource for all design and technology courses. A central book on **Designing** is complemented by books on **Communicating Design, Materials and Components,** and **Technology**. Within a broad range of contexts, these four student books present design and technological knowledge, concepts and techniques in a lively and accessible way.

Designing is the core book in the series. Using examples from the worlds of fashion, engineering and graphic design (to name just a few) as well as from school, it shows students how to explore and investigate contexts so as to identify needs and opportunities for designing. Practical advice is provided on imaging and generating design proposals and developing them into artefacts or systems. Throughout the book, students are encouraged to evaluate their work at each stage and to assess the designs of others.

Communicating Design shows students how to use a wide variety of techniques and media and helps them choose the best method of communicating their design ideas. Ranging from basic drawing techniques and the effective use of colour to methods of modelling in 3D, this book shows students how to achieve stunning effects cheaply and simply.

Materials and Components helps students choose appropriate materials and components for their project work. It relates the uses of different materials to their properties, providing a wealth of information and guidance on using ceramics, textiles, plastics and other 'modern' materials as well as wood and metal.

Technology covers the key areas of energy, energy sources, systems, structures and mechanisms. It gives students practical guidance on using technological systems in their project work, and looks at the wider applications and implications of technology both now and in the past.

A **Teacher's Resource Pack** provides a wealth of practical advice for teachers. It includes a substantial bank of photocopiable project briefs, linked to work in the students' books, and a wide range of stimulus material as a basis for class discussion with suggested discussion points.

Design and Technology in Action is a flexible series which will support the work of your GCSE students and provide an excellent resource for National Curriculum courses in design and technology.

About Communicating Design . . .

This book will help you learn how to communicate your design ideas. Throughout the design process you need to be able to express your ideas graphically – not just to show other people what you are doing but also to develop and test your ideas.

Communicating Design shows you how to use a wide variety of techniques, ranging from basic drawing and the effective use of colour to methods of model making in 3D. It will also help you choose the best way to present your design ideas – the first step towards a good exam grade.

. . . and how to use it

Use the book for reference when you are designing. It will help you find the best way of showing different stages of your design. Alternatively you can use the book as part of a course, working through the range of techniques.

The contents list on the next two pages and the index at the end of the book show you what the book covers and where to find it. And you can also use the colour-coded contents on the cover. The glossary at the back of the book will help you learn the essential working vocabulary.

Special features of this book

The techniques you need to know are clearly laid out in two-page units with close links between the illustrations and the text. Questions in each unit help you understand the techniques described on the page, and further questions and activities at the end of each section will help you apply your skills in new situations.

Contents

1 **Who communicates design ideas?** *1*

1.1 Design at Rover Group (I) *2*
1.2 Design at Rover Group (II) *4*
1.3 The design studio *6*
1.4 Tools of the designer's trade *8*
1.5 A design problem solved (I) *10*
1.6 A design problem solved (II) *12*
Exercises on chapter 1 14

◁**1**▷ *This chapter shows you some examples of how designers work and the tools they use.*

2 **Basic drawing techniques** *15*

2.1 Start drawing – with lines and boxes *16*
2.2 Drawing in context and perspective *18*
2.3 Slices, plans and elevations *20*
2.4 Perspectives, plans and planometrics *22*
2.5 More about orthographic drawings *24*
2.6 Communicating shape and detail *26*
2.7 Drawing curves and circles *28*
2.8 Making accurate drawings *30*
2.9 Looking inside an object *32*
2.10 How things fit together *34*
Exercises on chapter 2 36

◁**2**▷ *You will need to use drawing to show people your design ideas. This chapter will help you improve your drawing skills.*

◁**3**▷ *This chapter shows you how to make the best use of colour in your drawings.*

3 **Using colours and textures** *37*

3.1 Why use colour in drawings? *38*
3.2 Effective colouring techniques (I) *40*
3.3 Effective colouring techniques (II) *42*
3.4 Filling in the background *44*
3.5 Sprays in the studio *46*
3.6 Showing what it's made of *48*
3.7 Extra help for the designer *50*
Exercises on chapter 3 52

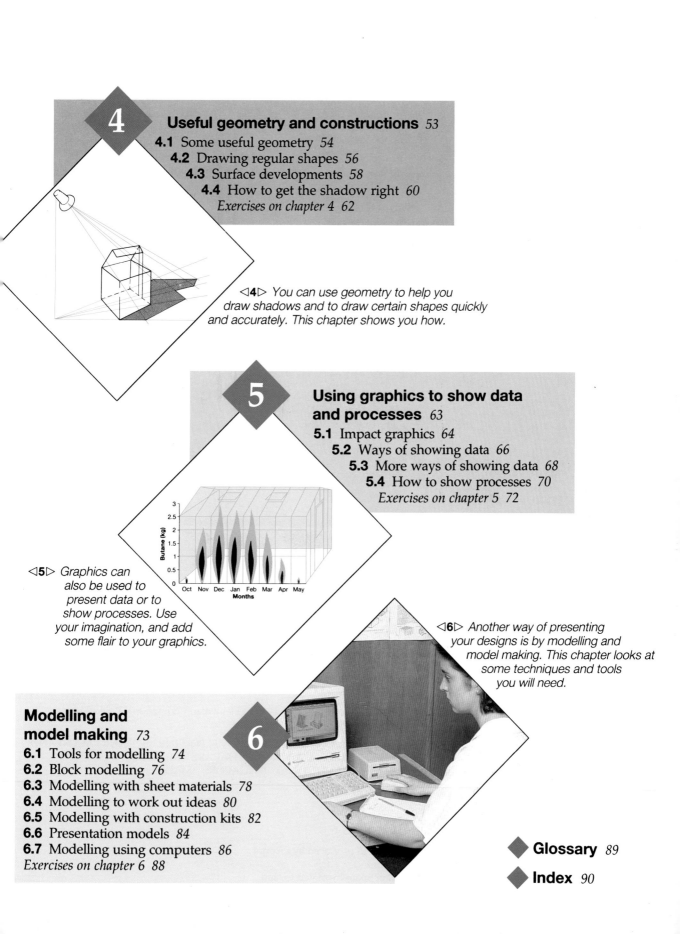

4 Useful geometry and constructions 53

4.1 Some useful geometry *54*
4.2 Drawing regular shapes *56*
4.3 Surface developments *58*
4.4 How to get the shadow right *60*
Exercises on chapter 4 62

◁4▷ *You can use geometry to help you draw shadows and to draw certain shapes quickly and accurately. This chapter shows you how.*

5 Using graphics to show data and processes 63

5.1 Impact graphics *64*
5.2 Ways of showing data *66*
5.3 More ways of showing data *68*
5.4 How to show processes *70*
Exercises on chapter 5 72

◁5▷ *Graphics can also be used to present data or to show processes. Use your imagination, and add some flair to your graphics.*

◁6▷ *Another way of presenting your designs is by modelling and model making. This chapter looks at some techniques and tools you will need.*

Modelling and model making 73

6.1 Tools for modelling *74*
6.2 Block modelling *76*
6.3 Modelling with sheet materials *78*
6.4 Modelling to work out ideas *80*
6.5 Modelling with construction kits *82*
6.6 Presentation models *84*
6.7 Modelling using computers *86*
Exercises on chapter 6 88

◆ **Glossary** *89*

◆ **Index** *90*

Acknowledgements

The publisher would like to thank the following for permission to reproduce photographs:

Argos 6.6.3; Keith Atkinson/Luton Architectural Models 2.4.2; British Museum 3.1.1; Richard Bryant/Arcaid 6.3.4; Caradon Mira Ltd 3.1.6; Sally & Richard Greenhill p.72, p.88; Robert Harding Picture Library 1.1.1; LEGO Group 6.5.4; MFI 2.10.3; Pictor International p.1; Michael Prior Studios 1.3.1, 1.3.2, 1.3.3, 1.3.4, 1.3.5, 1.6.7, p.14, 2.1.6, 2.1.9, 2.6.1, 2.7.1, 2.8.1, 2.8.4, 2.10.1, 2.10.2, 3.2.2, 3.2.3, 3.3.2, 3.5.1, 3.5.5, p.52, 4.2.1, 4.2.2, 4.3.1, 4.3.2, 6.1.1, 6.1.2, 6.1.3, 6.1.4, 6.1.5, 6.2.5, 6.3.2, 6.4.1, 6.5.1, 6.5.5, 6.6.1, 6.6.2, 6.6.4, p.88; Chris Ridgers Photography 1.3 (i–v), 1.6, p.14, 2.9.1, 3.2.2, 3.2.3, 3.3.2, 3.5.1, 3.5.5, p.52, p.73, 6.1.1, 6.1.2, 6.1.3, 6.1.4, 6.1.5, 6.2.5, 6.3.3; Alan Joiner/Rover Group 1.1.2, 1.1.3, 1.1.4, 1.1.5, 1.2.1, 1.2.2, 1.2.3, 1.2.4, 1.2.5, 1.2.6; UK Atomic Energy Authority, Culham Laboratory 3.1.5; Tom Ellaway 6.6.2.

Other photographs by Tom Baird.

The author would also like to thank the Head and pupils of Fitzharrys School, Abingdon.

Heinemann Educational, a division of Heinemann Educational Books Ltd, Halley Court, Jordan Hill, Oxford OX2 8EJ

OXFORD LONDON EDINBURGH MELBOURNE SYDNEY AUCKLAND IBADAN NAIROBI GABORONE HARARE KINGSTON PORTSMOUTH NH (USA) SINGAPORE MADRID

© Tom Baird 1990

First published 1990

ISBN 0 435 75001 1

Designed and produced by Oxprint Ltd, Oxford
Printed in Spain by Mateu Cromo

Who communicates design ideas?

Not all design studios are the same because not all designers use the same equipment. For example, a car designer needs different equipment from a book designer. This chapter shows you some examples of how designers work and the tools they use.

Design at Rover Group (I)

Developing design ideas

Sections 1.1 and 1.2 show you how car body designs are developed by the Rover Group. They don't tell you the whole story. Every part of a car, from the engine down to the nuts and bolts that hold it together, has been designed by someone. It would take several books to tell you about the whole process.

These sections also show you some of the ways car designers communicate their design ideas to other people. Rover use these methods because they are accurate and effective. This book will help *you* choose accurate and effective methods to communicate your own design ideas.

◁**1**▷ Market researchers question the public to find a gap in the market for a new car.

Identifying a need

First, market researchers try to find out what sort of new car would sell well ◁1▷. They ask a large number of people questions about what they would use a new car for, and how much they would spend on it. Then they **analyze** the answers – they look for patterns. For example, they may find out how much most people would pay for a four door family car.

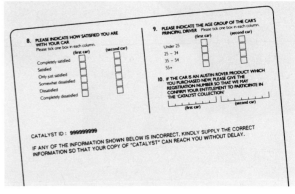

◁**2**▷ Forms like this are used to record information about what people need from a car.

Creating a design brief

The results of the market research are presented to the company's board of directors. The board use the results to help them decide what type of new car to make. They create a **design brief** which tells their designers about the features, style and cost of the car they want.

Initial design ideas

The next step is for the designers to produce **concept drawings** based on the brief ◁3▷. These are artist's impressions of the new car. The artists will show several different concept drawings to the directors.

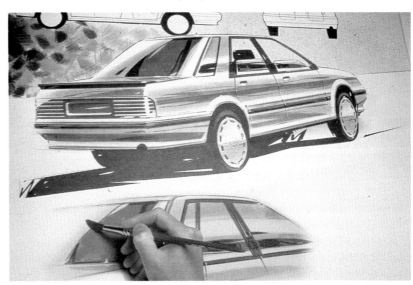

◁**3**▷ This **concept drawing** is an artist's impression based on the directors' design brief.

Presenting ideas in 3 D

When suitable concept drawings have been chosen, a full-sized clay model of the car is made. Now people can look at or touch the model from all sides, and see the details of the design. This helps to give an accurate impression of the design idea, and gives the designers a 'feel' for the car.

Sometimes full-sized glass fibre models of cars are made and shown to the public at a **design clinic** ◁4▷. This is a way of finding out which design people like best.

◁4▷ A **design clinic**. Full-size glass fibre models are shown to the public, who write down what they like and dislike about each one.

The final body design

When a final design has been chosen, its measurements are taken electronically and stored in a computer. The machine in ◁5▷ does this as it moves across the surface of the full-size clay model. The measurements are turned into numbers. This is called **digitizing**.

Rover keep the digitized information in their engineering database. A **database** is a store of information in a computer. Section 1.2 shows how the designers use this information.

◁5▷ This machine is **digitizing** (converting into numbers) the shape of the chosen clay design.

1 How do Rover find out what sort of car people will want to buy?

2 This section describes several ways of showing what a car is like. Write down as many of these as you can.

3 Most companies design things that people will want to buy. Can you think of anything which is designed and made, but *not* sold?

Design at Rover Group (II)

Mathematical model motor car

Rover Group's engineering database contains digital information about each car. The digits (numbers) give an accurate description of the shape of the car's bodywork – the length, height and thickness of each part, and how curved it is. The designers can make the computer produce different types of pictures from this **mathematical model**. It can display them on a screen. ◁1▷ and ◁2▷ are examples.

Wire-frame diagrams

◁1▷ is a wire-frame diagram of a car. The database holds digital information about each wire. The computer can show you the car in a different position by calculating the new position of each wire in turn. This lets the designer look at the car from any angle.

More realistic pictures

The designer can also make the computer shade in the spaces between the wires in the wire-frame diagram ◁2▷. This makes the car body look more realistic, and helps other people understand the diagram. It is important that others understand a designer's work. Section 6.7 shows you a computer being used in this way in a school.

Printing the pictures on paper

A **plotter** takes the screen image from the computer and makes a **hard copy** on paper ◁3▷. Hard copy just means it won't disappear when the computer is turned off. This type of drawing could be done by a person skilled in technical drawing, but the plotter does it faster. A good designer always uses the fastest and most accurate way of showing ideas, with the equipment available.

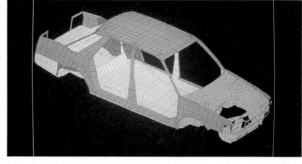

◁1▷ *This computer-generated* **wire-frame diagram** *shows the shape of the car body.*

◁2▷ *A computer-generated 3 D picture of the car body produced from information in the engineering database.*

◁3▷ *This* **plotter** *connected to the computer produces a full sized 2 D drawing of the car. The final drawing is very accurate.*

Working out ideas

As well as drawing pictures, computers can help solve many design problems by showing how well a design will work. ◁4▷ shows how Rover, working with the Motor Industry Research Association, use a computer to design a safe seat belt. The pictures show what would happen in an accident. The designer can alter the anchor points of the seat belt, and the computer will then produce pictures showing the effects. These simple line diagrams and tables tell the designer what she wants to know clearly and effectively.

Ways of showing the final design

The final design can be shown to the public in many different ways. High quality artwork like ◁5▷ and ◁6▷ may be used. These pictures were painted by artists, but they are very realistic, almost like photographs. They show how high quality artwork can be used both to give technical information and to show how attractive the car will be.

◁4▷ *These computer-generated line drawings show the effect of changing the anchor points of the seat belts.*

Choosing how to communicate an idea

Sections 1.1 and 1.2 show some ways of communicating ideas used at Rover. They don't show every method used, but they do show how important it is to have a range of ways of showing design ideas. Different ideas are best communicated in different ways. High quality artwork can give a customer a good idea of what a car looks like. It may not be the best way of telling a mechanic where all the engine parts are.

The Rover Group use both traditional art and craft skills and advanced computer-aided design to produce better designs and to communicate their design ideas.

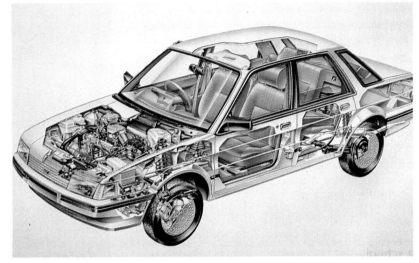

◁5▷ *This high quality **cut-away drawing** shows the positions of various car parts.*

1 Almost all the illustrations in sections 1.1 and 1.2 use colour. In which ones do you think this is most important, and why?
2 ◁5▷ and ◁6▷ are both important in putting across the image of the car. What image do you think the Rover Group want each of these cars to have?
3 Next time you see a car advert, try to work out who the car is supposed to appeal to.

◁6▷ *This high quality artwork shows potential customers the car's image.*

The design studio

What is a design studio?

A design studio is a place where designers work, and where they keep the equipment and resources they need to help them design. Designers specialize in different types of design problems and this makes design studios different from each other. The pictures on these pages were taken in a school design studio. All school design studios are different. This one is fairly well equipped.

Tackling design problems

When you design something new, or alter the design of something that already exists, you are tackling a design problem. You could be redesigning something to make it safer, or to make it look or work better. You might be designing something to make life easier, more interesting or more organized. A design studio should contain information to help you do this – **design resources**.

What are design resources?

Reference books, magazines, photographs, pictures and models are all useful resource materials. When you are designing, gather information to help you solve problems from the resources in the studio. For example, you will need information on:

- properties of materials
- processes – ways of working with materials
- science and technology – how things work
- nature's solutions to problems – examples from plants and animals
- current fashions and trends
- how to generate design ideas

You should also know where to look for more information *outside* the design studio. Companies, libraries and museums will all have information you can use.

A good place to design

A design studio should be: stimulating, tidy, clean, comfortable, colourful, well-lit and ventilated. A wide variety of jobs are done in a design studio. Because of this it should be organized so people can concentrate on their work, but also move about and discuss ideas when they need to. For this to work you need to show respect for other designers you work with, even when your own designs are not working out well!

◁3▷

What will you do in the design studio?

Here are some of the things you will do using the equipment and resources in the design studio:

Researching and discussing: Collect information to help you solve design problems from the resources in the studio. Discuss your solutions with other people.

Using graphics: Get your ideas down on paper so you can show them to others. You will need the equipment and skills to do this in a variety of ways.

Evaluating: This is judging how effective a design idea is. You should be evaluating your design ideas all the time, and seeing if you can alter them to improve them. Keep a note of the changes you make as they will help you with future designs.

Using electronic and photographic aids: Find out about equipment which makes it easier to design (e.g. cameras, photocopiers and computers). Only use this equipment if it makes your task easier or improves the quality of your work.

Making sketch models: Make models of parts of your designs that you can't show well on paper. For this you will need a 'dirty work' area – away from clean drawing surfaces and computers.

Making prototypes: Prototypes are very accurately made models. Some of your designs may have to be taken to prototype stage to communicate your ideas fully.

Making a resource folder: Store your finished work *and* your initial design work in a resource folder. If you can, keep photographs of any models you make there too. All your work adds to the knowledge you bring to your next design problem, so it is very valuable.

---

1 Study the design activities shown in the pictures. For each one, write down what you think the people are doing and why.
2 A list of design activities is given on this page. To help plan the best use of your time, make a table like the one on the right. In your table, write down which activities could be done in each place.

at home	at school	in both places

Tools of the designer's trade

Materials and equipment for designing

You don't need all the equipment shown on this page to design. You can work out solutions to many design problems with just a pencil and paper. But to show your ideas to other people, a pencil and paper may not be enough. Different ideas will need to be presented in different ways. You will have to choose the best way, using the equipment and materials you have available.

In the design studio you can use equipment in many different ways to help people understand your design ideas. Experiment with equipment to find new and better ways of using it. For example, pastel dust and lighter fuel can be used together to make an attractive background for an illustration (details in section 3.4). Look at the equipment in the drawing. You will find these items in most studios.

The materials and equipment in the picture

See if you can find each of these items shown in the picture:

drawing board	set square	protractor
french curve	flexicurve	ellipse template
scale rule	scissors	pencil sharpener
scalpel and knife	pencil	eraser
crayon	pastels	cotton wool
gouache (paint)	Kuretake (fineliner)	Stabilayout (marker)
masking tape	lighter fuel (solvent)	drawing board clip
Spray Mount (glue)	Spray Fix (fixative)	compass
Pelifix (glue)	talcum powder	Majicolor (ink)
paint brushes	word processor	Pelikan ink

Some basic illustration techniques

The equipment in the picture is mainly used to present ideas on paper. Here are some techniques that designers use to do this:

Sketching: a quick but accurate drawing with only a few lines

Colour rendering: adding colour to draw attention or improve appearance

Highlighting and shading: adding brightness and shadow to indicate shape and texture

Cut and paste: cutting out and repositioning drawings or words on a page to get a better arrangement

Masking: covering areas to protect the work underneath from colour applied later

Fixing: spraying on a protective coating to prevent smudging

Drawing with instruments: for very accurate work

◁1▷ *This **pen and ink sketch** shows just some of the wide range of equipment used in a school design studio. Sketching is a quick but accurate way of communicating this information.*

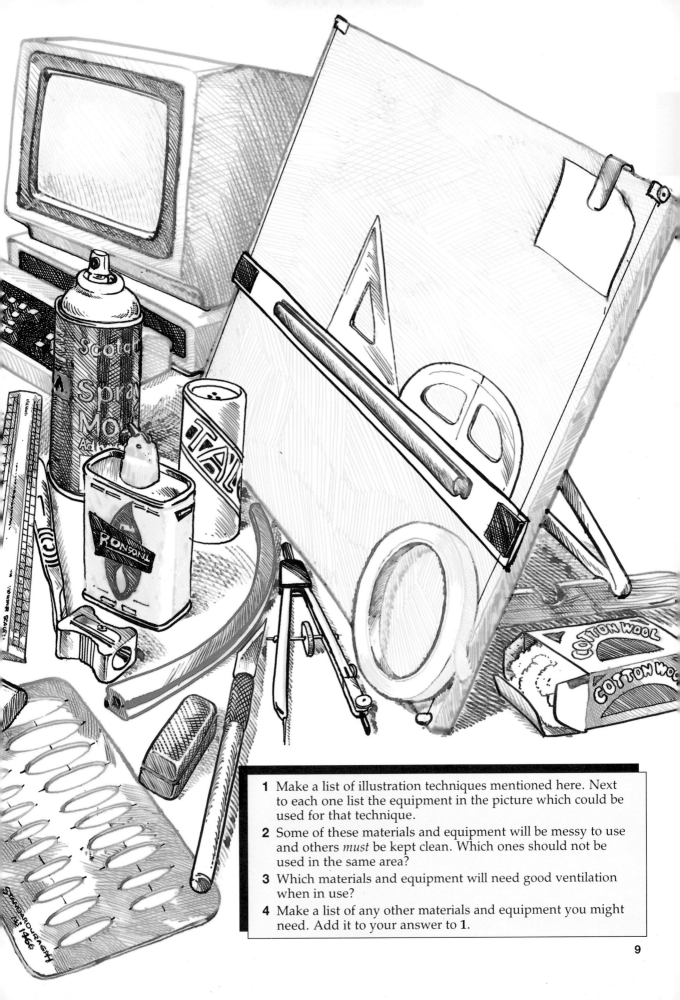

1 Make a list of illustration techniques mentioned here. Next to each one list the equipment in the picture which could be used for that technique.
2 Some of these materials and equipment will be messy to use and others *must* be kept clean. Which ones should not be used in the same area?
3 Which materials and equipment will need good ventilation when in use?
4 Make a list of any other materials and equipment you might need. Add it to your answer to 1.

A design problem solved (I)

Design drawings for a mechanical toy

Here is a set of design drawings for the toy duck shown in ◁1▷. The designer was given a **design brief** which asked her to design a clockwork toy using the motor shown in one of the drawings. These are just some of the drawings she did to help work out and show her ideas. They are not shown in any particular order, but see if you can work out which order they were drawn in. Here are some clues:

- Look out for the drawing in which she **analyzed** the motor to see how it would affect the design. The toy cannot be smaller than the motor. This is a **constraint** – something she cannot change.
- Look for drawings of her **initial** (first) ideas. Find out where the duck idea first appeared.
- Look for pictures that **develop** the duck idea.
- Where did the designer start working out how the toy would be **made**?
- Which drawing do you think she made last?
- Some drawings are to 'show off' or **present** the idea to the person who set the brief. Which ones are these?

◁1▷

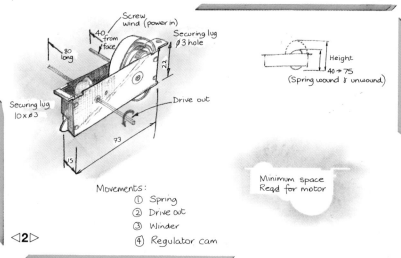

Minimum space Reqd for motor

Movements:
① Spring
② Drive out
③ Winder
④ Regulator cam

◁2▷

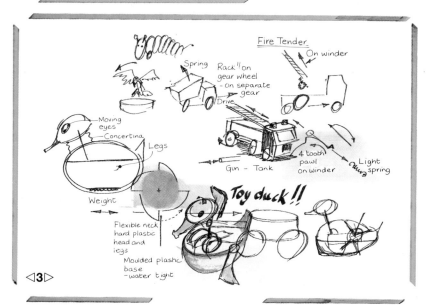

◁3▷

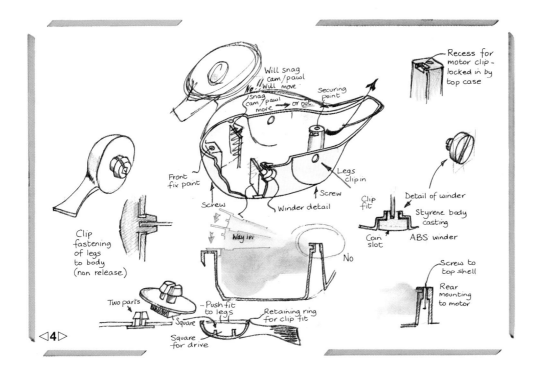

Will snag
cam/pawl
Will move

Snag
cam/pawl
move → or out

Securing
point

Recess for
motor clip -
locked in by
top case

Front
fix point

Legs
clip in

Screw

Screw

Winder detail

Clip
fit

Detail of winder

Styrene body
casting

ABS winder

Coin
slot

Clip
fastening
of legs
to body
(non release.)

Way in

No

Screw to
top shell

Rear
mounting
to motor

Two parts

Push fit
to legs

Square

Retaining ring
for clip fit

Square
for drive

◁**4**▷

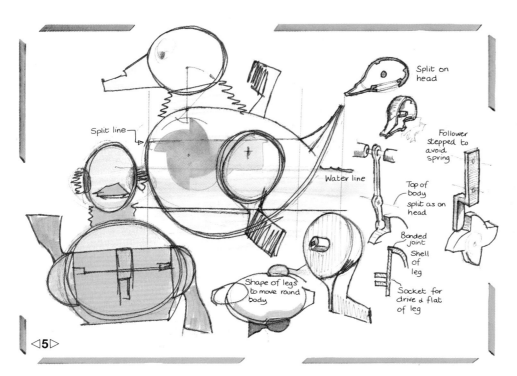

Split on
head

Split line

Follower
stepped to
avoid
spring

Water line

Top of
body
split as on
head

Bonded
joint

Shell
of
leg

Shape of legs
to move round
body

Socket for
drive & flat
of leg

◁**5**▷

1 Write down the order you think these pictures were made in. For each drawing write down what you think the designer was trying to do.

    The box at the bottom of page 14 tells you what the designer thought she was doing!

2 Make a list of the equipment you think she used to do these drawings.

A design problem solved (II)

Designing a personal stereo case

Section 1.5 showed how a professional designer solved a design problem. This section shows you how Scott Osborne, a 14 year old student, solved another design problem. Here is the background information he was given:

A manufacturer has identified a need for a personal stereo for 11 to 12 year olds. The potential users are children who listen to pop music and story tapes. The manufacturers already make personal stereos for older users. They want to use the electronics and mechanism from an existing model, but redesign the case to appeal to younger users.

BLACK BOX
WITH WORKS

Heads slide forward

A – PLAY
B – REW
C – F FOR
D – STOP/EJECT

Push

ADD: Volume control
Jack socket
Battery holder

◁**1**▷ *The manufacturers want to make a new personal stereo using this mechanism.*

The design brief

Scott's teacher asked him to design a new case, following this design brief:

- it should appeal to 11 to 12 year olds
- it should use the mechanism shown in ◁1▷
- it should have a toy-like feel, but not look cheap
- it should withstand rough treatment

Gathering information

Scott collected quite a lot of information to help him solve this design problem. He looked at some children's toys to find out what appeals to 11–12 year olds. He also needed information about the dimensions (sizes) of the battery and the manufacturer's mechanism. ◁2▷ shows how he recorded this information to use while designing.

The size of the battery and the size of the stereo mechanism are **constraints** – things Scott cannot change. His design must take account of these constraints.

◁**2**▷ *Scott recorded the constraints on his design like this.*

◁**3**▷ *Scott's initial ideas for solutions to the design problem.*

Raised buttons

Recessed edge

Textured battery flap

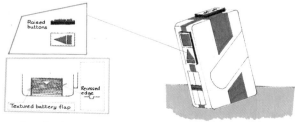

◁**4**▷ *Scott's chosen solution. These drawings show some details he wants to put on the case.*

From initial ideas . . . to a chosen solution

◁**3**▷ shows some of Scott's initial ideas for solutions to the design problem. And ◁**4**▷ shows the solution he chose, with some details he wanted to put on the case.

Accurate drawings of the solution

◁**5**▷ shows accurate views of three sides of Scott's personal stereo design. It shows the sizes and colours of the parts, and where they fit. ◁**6**▷ shows you the symbols to go on the buttons, earphone socket and battery compartment.

◁**5**▷ *This accurate drawing shows the sizes, positions and colours of the main parts of the case.*

◁**6**▷ *Drawings of the symbols to be used on the stereo.*

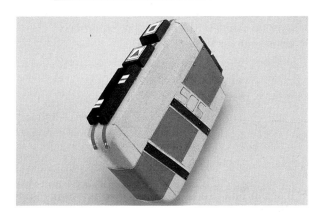

Battery Compartment Symbol

Rewind Button

Ear Phone Socket Symbol

Play Button

Fast Forward Button

Stop/ Eject Button

A model of the final design

◁**7**▷ shows Scott's full-size model of his design. He could have made a very realistic drawing of the stereo, but he thought a model would give people a better idea of the size and feel of his design, and generally show it off better. To make his model Scott used measurements from ◁**5**▷, and details from ◁**4**▷ and ◁**6**▷.

Evaluating the design

Evaluating means: judging how well something works. Scott evaluated his design to see how well it satisfied the original design brief. He explained the problems he encountered, and how he could improve his design. His evaluation is shown in ◁**8**▷.

◁**7**▷ *This full-size model gives you a good idea of the size, shape and appearance of Scott's design.*

PERSONAL STEREO

I believe that my design has solved the problem of making a personal stereo for the pre-teenage market. It had a toy quality but didn't look cheap. Because an existing mechanism was being used I only had to design the body work. The buttons are easily identified with large symbols, clear enough to be understood by a child. I have not put a particular identification mark like a transformer or care bear to show it is aimed at the pre-teenage market although I have used a trendy paint job.

◁**8**▷ *Part of Scott's evaluation in which he says how well he thinks his design satisfies the original brief.*

1 Scott made a model of his final design instead of a drawing. Why did he do this?

2 What is a constraint, and what were the constraints on Scott's stereo design?

3 Read Scott's evaluation in ◁**8**▷. How well do you think he solved the problem given in the design brief?

Exercises on chapter 1

1 Make a reference chart of all your felt tip pens and markers to show what colour they are when used on your normal drawing paper.

 • Label each marker with its name, and show the thickness of the nib when in normal use.
 • Store your chart in a folder so the colours won't be bleached by sunlight.

2 Magazines are a useful design resource. Design a system of displaying and storing magazines in your school design studio.

 • Produce some sketches to show how your system would look in the studio.
 • You could start with a photograph of the studio and draw your ideas on top of it.

3 Sometimes you will need to take equipment out of the design studio to make notes and sketches, or record information to help you solve a problem. Design an inexpensive container for this equipment.

 • Start by deciding what you would include in a portable set of equipment.
 • Imagine the types of places you might go for help, information or inspiration, and the equipment you may need when you are there.

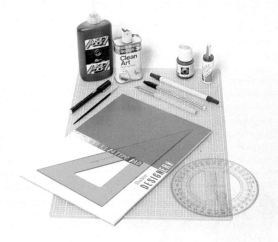

4 Your school design studio is a busy place used by many people. Devise a set of rules to encourage users to leave the studio in the same condition in which they would like to find it.

 • Start by listing all the things you find frustrating when they are not exactly as you like them in the studio.
 • Design a poster showing the rules which you think are the most important.

◁1▷ *This photograph may help you answer question 3.*

A design problem solved (I)

The designer of the toy duck in 1.5 went through these stages to help her work out and show her ideas:

1 She analyzed the motor and noted the constraints.
2 She looked for her initial ideas for a design.
3 She settled on a design and tried to work out the proportions.
4 She tried to work out how the final design would be made.
5 She presented her ideas to the manufacturer.

Basic drawing techniques

You will need to use drawings to show people your design ideas. Everyone can learn to draw but it takes practice. This chapter looks at different ways of showing what an object is like, and will help you improve your drawing skills.

Start drawing – with lines and boxes

Good drawing takes practice

If you were an athlete you would train for events. Designers have to do the same with drawing skills to enable them to express their designs. A good tennis player is so practised in the strokes that he thinks only of the game. A good designer is so practised in drawing that she thinks only of her design as her hand draws. You can learn to draw, just as you can learn to ride a bike. Some people do it better than others, but *everyone can draw.*

Drawing lines easily

The three types of lines shown below are called **natural lines**.

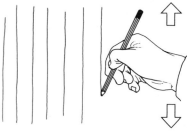

◁**1**▷ Some lines are easier to draw than others. These lines are easier for right-handed people to draw.

◁**2**▷ These lines are easier for left-handed people to draw. To draw slanting lines, start with the pen near the middle of your body and move it away from you.

◁**3**▷ Vertical lines (up and down) need more practice. To draw them, keep your hand to one side, so you can see the tip of your pen, pencil or brush.

Ghosting lines

You can have a trial run before you draw a line. Move your pen backwards and forwards in the direction of the line, with the pen *only just touching the paper.* This useful technique is called **ghosting**. When the line looks right, draw it boldly.

Moving the paper

If you find it hard to draw some lines, turn the paper to a more comfortable angle for drawing them. This may slow you down, but it will make drawing easier. Eventually you will be able to draw without turning the paper. You probably won't notice when you change!

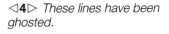

◁**4**▷ These lines have been ghosted.

Drawing boxes

You can use natural lines to draw boxes. When you start a sketch, get the direction of each line right before you fix its length.

▷ Rule: direction first, length second ◁

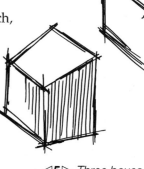

Ghost your lines, putting one faint line on top of another. Don't draw a heavy line until the ghosted box looks right. One of my boxes in ◁**5**▷ is badly drawn. If you can tell which box looks wrong, you won't have trouble seeing mistakes in your own drawings.

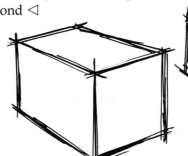

◁**5**▷ Three boxes drawn with natural lines. Which box looks wrong?

Use boxes to help you draw

You can use boxes to help you draw more complicated shapes. Here's how to draw a J cloth pack.

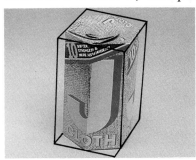

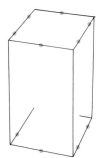

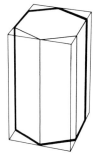

◁**6**▷ *First look at the pack and imagine a guide box around it. Draw this box at the viewing angle you want. Don't draw anything else until the box looks right.*

◁**7**▷ *Find the points where the pack touches the box. Add these points to your drawing.*

◁**8**▷ *Join the points together to make a drawing of the box at the correct viewing angle.*

Getting things in proportion

Remember: you must look at the object you are drawing to see what shape the guide box should be. If the object won't fit inside your box, you won't draw it correctly. The box may have to be six times as long as it is high, or almost as wide as it is long. The relationships between its length, width and height are known as the **proportions** of the box.

◁**9**▷ *The proportions of your guide box depend on the shape you want to draw.*

Making drawings look solid

The shapes in ◁**10**▷ are **prisms**. They were drawn using the **thick and thin line** technique which makes objects look more solid. It shows you the **form** (shape) of an object. Add thick and thin lines after ghosting the shape.

Follow these rules:

▷ When you can see the surfaces on both sides of an edge, draw that edge **thin**.

▷ When you are looking over an edge into space or onto the ground, draw the edge **thick**.

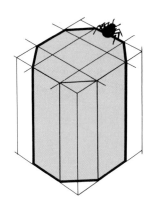

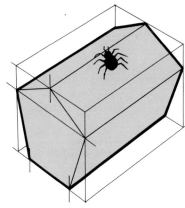

◁**10**▷ ***Thick and thin lines*** *make these prisms look more solid. Imagine a spider walking over the edges. If she walks over an edge and vanishes, draw it thick. If you can still see her, draw it thin.*

1 Look at all the boxes in the pictures. You are looking *down* on them. Now draw some that you look *up* to.
2 In ◁**5**▷ one box is shaded to show its form. Draw the prisms from ◁**10**▷ and add shading to them.
3 The word *look* has been used many times here. You have to look before you draw. Look at a power socket in your design studio. Draw it in correct proportion.

Drawing in context and perspective

Drawing an object in context

This section shows you several different ways of drawing the same object. Each way tells you something about the object, but no one way tells you everything.

◁**1**▷ shows the object. It's rectangular, with a rough texture, and it is a pale red-brown colour. The picture doesn't give you enough clues to be sure what the object is. But you might be able to guess from its proportions, colour and texture.

◁**2**▷ shows the object **in context** (in its normal surroundings). Even though the viewing angle is the same as in ◁**1**▷, now it is easier to tell that the object is a brick.

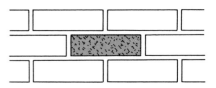

◁**1**▷ It's hard to tell what this object is because it's drawn out of context – it's normal surroundings aren't shown.

Drawing realistic views

◁**3**▷ shows the brick both in context *and* drawn at a realistic viewing angle. It's easier to recognize things when they are drawn the way you usually see them – at an angle rather than flat on. A realistic drawing like this is called a **perspective drawing** – this is a drawing on a flat surface which creates the illusion of depth.

Compare ◁**2**▷ and ◁**3**▷. Notice how the horizontal lines between the bricks in ◁**2**▷ look different in ◁**3**▷. In ◁**3**▷ these lines appear to **converge** (get closer together) as they get further away from you. If you extended these lines further they would appear to meet each other and vanish at two **vanishing points** on the **horizon line** – the line separating the sky from the ground. A drawing with two vanishing points is called a **two-point perspective**. Notice that vertical lines do not converge in the drawing.

◁**2**▷ Now the object is **in context** – it's part of a wall, so it must be a brick.

Horizon   Vanishing point

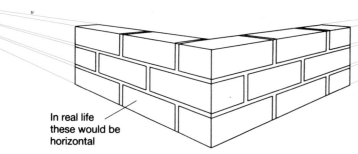

In real life these would be horizontal

◁**3**▷ In a two-point perspective drawing, lines **converge** towards two **vanishing points**.

Sketching a brick in two-point perspective

V.P.   Horizon line   V.P. V.P.   V.P.V.P.   V.P.

◁**4**▷ Draw a horizon line with a vanishing point at each end. Ghost a vertical line below it to represent the front corner of the brick.

◁**5**▷ Next ghost lines from the front corner to the vanishing points. When the directions look right mark the lengths of the brick's sides.

◁**6**▷ Now draw the other edges in and add the details. Hint: you can draw the hollow in the top of the brick by ghosting lines to the vanishing points.

Getting the proportions and size right

◁7▷ is another two-point perspective. This drawing does not show lines converging to the vanishing points, but the brick 'looks right'. I have judged its shape by eye. With practice you will be able to do this too. You will know that your drawings are accurate when they look right.

A perspective sketch like ◁7▷ lets you show an object quickly. It gives an idea of the **proportions** of the object – how big one side is compared with another. By adding **dimension lines** and **measurements** (in millimetres), you can show the true size of the object.

100 mm

175 mm

Dimension lines

70 mm

215 mm

◁7▷ *Dimension lines* and *measurements* on this rough sketch tell you how big the brick is.

Is it above you or below you?

Two-point perspective allows you to show whether an object is above you, below you, or level with you. The horizon line in your drawing is level with your eye. If the object is above your eye, you draw it above the horizon line. If it's below your eye you draw it below the horizon line ◁8▷.

◁8▷ *To show an object above (or below) you, draw it above (or below) the horizon line.*

V.P.　　　　　　　　　　Horizon　　　　　　　　　　V.P.

Special effects

You can alter your viewing angle and the positions of the vanishing points to give your drawings visual impact. Try drawing an object quite far away from the horizon line – either above or below it. The further away it gets the more dramatic the effect ◁9▷.

◁9▷ *Here the vanishing points have been drawn close together to give an interesting effect.*

V.P.　　　　　　　　　Horizon　　　　　　　　　V.P.

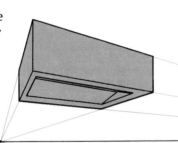

1 Write down your own explanations of these words and phrases. Use sketches if this helps.
   vanishing point
   horizon line
   two-point perspective
2 Draw a brick-built barbeque in two-point perspective. Show each brick and the layers of mortar clearly.
3 Make two drawings of a cereal box from different viewing angles, and with vanishing points in different positions. Make one box look realistic, and the other look as big as a building.

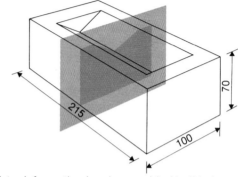

2.3
Slices, plans and elevations

Slicing to show a shape

◁1▷ is a two-point perspective of the brick from
section 2.2. The brick has a wedge-shaped
hollow in its top called a frog. To show the shape
of the frog, I have drawn a coloured **plane** slicing
through the brick. This draws attention to
something you might not have noticed
otherwise. As a designer you will often need to
draw attention to shapes like this.

Notice that if you extended lines from the top
and bottom edges of the plane they would meet
at a vanishing point on the horizon line. This
makes the drawing look neat.

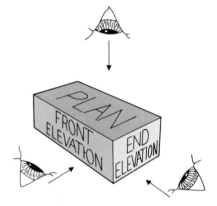

◁1▷ *Extra information has been added to this* **two
point perspective** *drawing to show the shape and
size of the brick.*

Looking straight at things – an orthographic view

An **orthographic view** is a view of something 'flat on'.
Section 2.2 ◁1▷ and ◁2▷ are examples of this. Now look again at
the drawing at the top of this page. It tells you quite a lot about the
brick, because it gives you some measurements and shows you
three sides. You could get the same information from *several*
orthographic views. One wouldn't be enough. Can you see why
not?

Showing several sides flat-on – an orthographic drawing

◁3▷ shows several drawings of the brick from different viewpoints.
A group of drawings like this is called an **orthographic drawing**.
Compare ◁1▷ and ◁3▷ and see how the same information has
been presented differently.

Each view in an orthographic drawing has a name. Look
carefully at ◁3▷ and see if you can spot how the **front elevation,
end elevation** and **plan** are related to each other. ◁2▷ will help.

◁2▷ **Orthographic views**
*made from each of these positions
are shown in* ◁3▷.

◁3▷ *An* **orthographic
drawing** *shows several
views from different positions.
It gives accurate information
about the size, shape and
proportions of an object.*

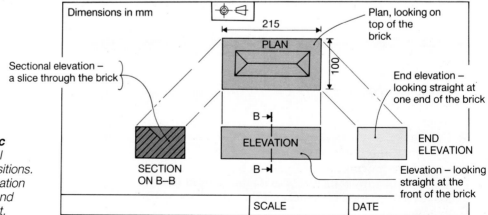

20

Third angle or first angle?

◁4▷ and ◁5▷ show you two different orthographic projections of the same object.

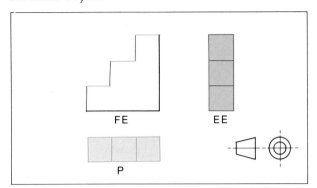

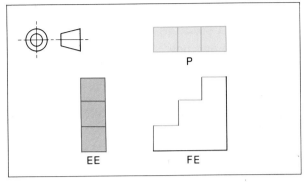

◁4▷ *In first angle orthographic projection, draw the front elevation (FE) and then draw the end elevation (EE) beyond and level with it. Draw the plan (P) beyond and below the front elevation.*

◁5▷ *In third angle orthographic projection, draw the end elevation (EE) in front of and level with the front elevation (FE). Draw the plan (P) in line with and above the front elevation.*

Using instruments for formal drawings

The orthographic drawing in ◁3▷ was made using drawing instruments. All the lines are straight and the lengths are accurate. The top and bottom edges of the brick have been drawn at right angles to each other. ◁6▷ shows you how to do this quickly and easily using a **T square** and a **set square**. These drawing instruments slide over the surface of the paper so they must be kept clean. To stop the paper sliding too, attach it firmly to the board with clips ◁6▷.

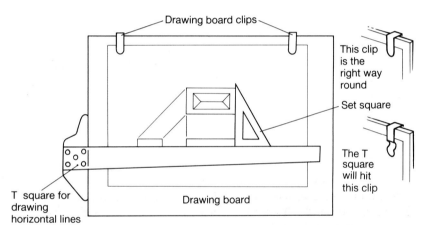

◁6▷ *A **T square** and **set square** help you draw straight horizontal and vertical lines. An accurate drawing made with instruments is sometimes called a **formal** drawing.*

---

1 Two drawing styles are shown in this section: **two point perspective** and **orthographic projection**. Write brief notes to say which style would be most suitable for each of these drawings:
- to show what a microwave oven looks like
- to show a builder the shape and size of a new garage
- to show the amount of carpet needed for a flat

2 Sketch or trace the objects shown on the right. Then draw a plane through each one and shade the area where the plane cuts through the object.

3 Draw a carton of fruit juice in two ways:
- in orthographic projection to show the size
- in two point perspective, showing the maker's name or any other surface details

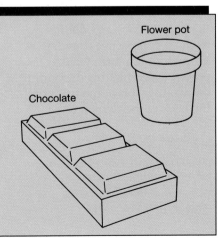

Flower pot

Chocolate

Perspectives, plans and planometrics

Choosing a suitable drawing method

Section 2.2 shows how you can use two point perspective and orthographic projection to show different aspects of the same idea. An experienced designer can convert from one of these systems of drawing to the other in her head. When given a two point perspective, she can **visualize** (see in her head) what an orthographic projection of the same object will look like. But not everyone can do this. To get an idea across to someone else, the designer must choose the most suitable method. This section shows you some useful methods.

An architect can look at plans and elevations like those in 3.1 ◁**3**▷ and picture the house in his head. But a buyer might find it easier to understand a two point perspective like ◁**1**▷. Sometimes a model like ◁**2**▷ may be better than a drawing.

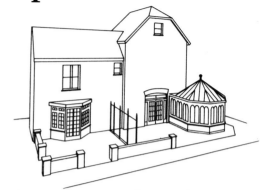

◁**1**▷ *A **two point perspective** can give you a good idea of what a house will look like when it is built.*

◁**2**▷ *A model can get complex ideas across quickly.*

Single point perspective

◁**3**▷ shows four bricks drawn in **single point perspective**. It's called this because there is only a *single* vanishing point on the horizon. You can see the construction lines converging towards it. When you draw a single point perspective, choose your viewpoint carefully. Two of the bricks in ◁**3**▷ look odd because they are badly positioned.

In single point perspective the front of an object is drawn flat on to the viewer. If the scale of the drawing is given, you can measure the size of the front of the object. You can't do this from all perspective drawings – a 1 metre high bush will be drawn different sizes depending on whether it is at the front or the back of the drawing.

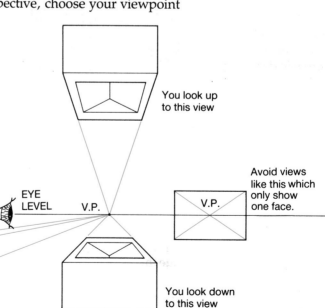

You look up to this view

Avoid views like this which only show one face.

EYE LEVEL   V.P.   V.P.

You look down to this view

◁**3**▷ *A **single point perspective** shows an object 'flat on', but you need to choose your viewpoint carefully.*

Looking inside an object

You can use single point perspective to show the inside of an object. ◁4▷ shows what a room in a house would look like with the wall nearest you removed. You can see the construction lines converging towards the vanishing point on the horizon.

Showing sizes and proportions

◁4▷ gives a good impression of what a room is like. But you couldn't use this one point perspective to tell a heating engineer exactly where to put a radiator, or an electrician where to put a power point. You *could* do this with the **elevations** and **plan** in ◁5▷.

Four elevations are shown in ◁5▷ – one for each side of the room. They are labelled north, south, east and west to show which way you are looking. The plan and elevations are drawn to scale, so accurate measurements can be taken from these drawings. Used together, ◁4▷ and ◁5▷ tell you a lot about the room. (See also section 2.3).

Planometric drawings

The information in the plans and elevations can be used to make a **planometric drawing** as in ◁6▷. It is called planometric because it starts with an accurate *plan* like the one in ◁5▷. The plan is turned through an angle (30° in the one shown here), then details from the elevations are added. All real-life verticals are shown as vertical lines, and *all* lines are drawn accurately to scale.

Like a perspective drawing, a planometric drawing does give you some idea of the shape of the room. But you can make accurate measurements from a planometric drawing because all the lines are drawn to scale.

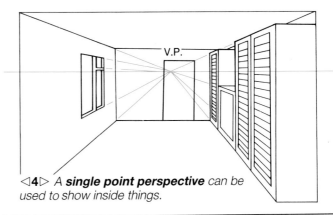

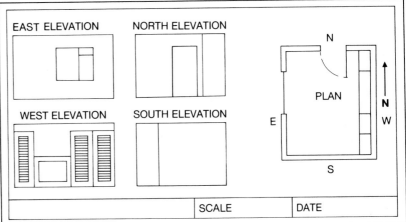

◁4▷ A **single point perspective** can be used to show inside things.

◁5▷ **Plans** and **elevations** give accurate information about the size and proportions of this room.

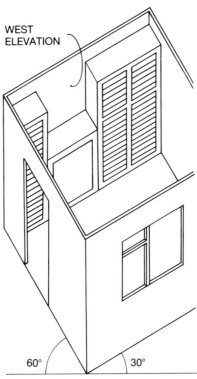

◁6▷ A **planometric projection** made from the plan in ◁5▷.

1 In 2.3 ◁3▷ a sectional elevation was labelled 'section on B–B'. How and why have the elevations on this page been labelled?

2 Write brief notes to explain which of these drawings you could measure sizes from:
   • two point perspective
   • planometric
   • single point perspective
   • orthographic

3 Middlebridge Council are planning a new sports centre. Which types of drawings should they use to show users what it will look like inside and out?

4 Use two different methods to show what a blackboard rubber is like.

More about orthographic drawings

Remember the rules

Orthographic drawing is a way of showing objects as though you were looking at them 'flat on'. These drawings show shapes and sizes accurately so you can use them to show exactly what an object is like.

You have to obey complicated **conventions** (rules) when you make an orthographic drawing. These help other people to understand what you have drawn. This section shows you some of the orthographic conventions so that you can start doing these drawings yourself. Make your orthographic drawings as accurate as you can. Someone may want to make what you have drawn.

Types of lines used

Outline

Construction line

Hidden edge lines

Chain lines or centre lines

Marking sizes on drawings

Notice how construction lines and dimension lines are positioned.

Measurements are printed *above* dimension lines, reading from either the bottom or the right-hand edge of the page.

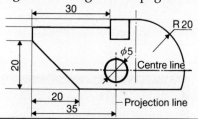

Title box and parts list

Drawings should always include a title, number, date and scale, with the name of the person who did the drawing. The parts included in the drawing should be listed.

	N°	PART	MATERIAL
NAME:	TITLE:	DATE:	DRG N°:

SECTION ON B–B

WEB 10

R10

φ6

φ12

φ9

30°

60

80

B   B

BRACKET	SCALE 1:1	DATE 22/7/88

First angle orthographic projection

The colours show how the pictorial view is related to the orthographic projection.

Third angle orthographic projection

Notice how this drawing differs from the first angle projection.

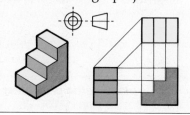

Projection symbols

3rd angle orthographic

1st angle orthographic

Abbreviations

Abbreviations are useful for saving time and avoiding clutter on drawings. Here are some useful ones:

M.S.	Mild steel	M20	20 mm metric thread
C.I.	Cast iron	A/F	Across flats
CRS	Centres	A/C	Across corners
R	Radius	C'BORE	Counter bore
φ	Diameter	CSK	Counter sink
▽	Machined	THRO'	Through

Sections

These are views of slices through an object. Different parts of an object are shown **hatched** (shaded) in different directions.

Orthographic conventions say that you don't show sections through nuts, bolts, screws, shafts and webs.

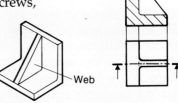

A →

A →

Section on A–A

Web

Showing hidden details with sections

Imagine a cut through the middle of the object. Hatch (shade) the parts that are cut. Remember: don't hatch webs.

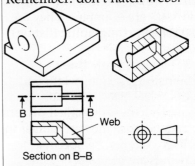

B   B

Web

Section on B–B

Dotted lines show hidden details

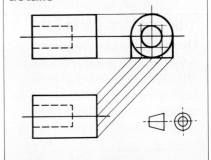

3	M20	WASHER	M.S.
3	M20	SCREW	M.S.
N°	PART		
DRG N°			

Showing nuts and bolts

D = diameter of thread

1.75 D
0.7 D
D
0.1 D
Radius = D
0.8 D

0.7 D 1.5 D
Round head

1.5 D
0.25 D
Cheese head

Countersunk

1 Copy the title box and margin style used on the centre drawing. Design an egg cup and draw it in first angle projection. Use a section to show the shape of the hollow.

2 Follow the rules on sizes of nuts and bolts, and draw each type with a diameter of 20 mm. In this case D = 20. Make sure you use the right types of lines.

3 Draw a pictorial sketch of the bracket in the central illustration. Show the section that cuts through B–B on your sketch.

Communicating shape and detail

Showing what an object is like

This section describes more ways of showing what an object is like. Compare the methods to find the best features of each one. And don't forget that you can use photographs to show colours, tones (brightness) and shapes. Include a ruler or a familiar object in a photograph and you can indicate sizes too, so you may not need to do a drawing.

◁**1**▷ *Sometimes a photograph is more suitable than a drawing. The ruler in this one shows you the scale.*

2 D or 3 D images

Two types of images are shown here. 2 D images show **two dimensions:** height and width. ◁**3**▷ and ◁**4**▷ are examples. They are also called **orthographic** (flat on) images.

3 D images show **three dimensions:** height, width and depth. ◁**2**▷, ◁**5**▷ and ◁**6**▷ are examples. These are called **pictorial** images because they are similar to realistic pictures. Perspective drawings are pictorial.

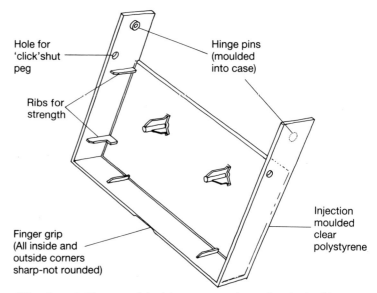

Hole for 'click'shut peg

Hinge pins (moulded into case)

Ribs for strength

Finger grip (All inside and outside corners sharp-not rounded)

Injection moulded clear polystyrene

Annotations give information

You can add **annotations** (notes) to your drawings to say what the different parts are, what they do, and what they are made from – see ◁**2**▷. When you do this you are **annotating** a drawing. Annotations can help you remember your thoughts when you next see the drawing.

◁**2**▷ **Annotations** *explain things you can't see just by looking.*

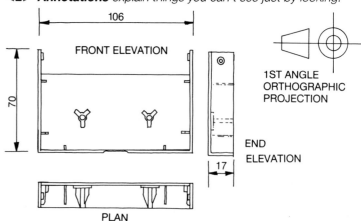

106

FRONT ELEVATION

70

1ST ANGLE ORTHOGRAPHIC PROJECTION

END ELEVATION

17

PLAN

Orthographic sketches

If you want to test an idea out on someone else, try doing an orthographic sketch like the one in ◁**3**▷. Section 2.3 ◁**4**▷ and ◁**5**▷ show you how to lay out first angle and third angle orthographic projections. You can lay a sketch out the same way, and it's quicker to draw than a formal orthographic projection.

◁**3**▷ *A sketch orthographic projection shows sizes and proportions, but it's quicker to draw than a formal orthographic projection.*

Getting down to details

When you have worked out a design idea you may want to give someone else enough information to be able to make it. A **detail drawing** like ◁**4**▷ carries enough information for the part to be manufactured. This is a formal (accurately drawn) orthographic projection. Sections 2.3 and 2.5 tell you more about this type of drawing.

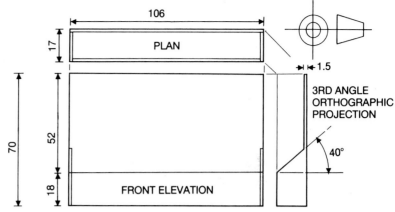

◁**4**▷ *This accurately drawn orthographic projection gives exact details about one part of the box. It is a **detail drawing**.*

Parallel pictorial projections

Parallel pictorial projections are 3 D drawings from which you can make accurate measurements. All lines are drawn to scale and they do not converge to a vanishing point. There are several different types of parallel pictorial projections:

Isometric projections – see ◁**5**▷. All lines (except verticals) are drawn at an angle of 30° to the horizontal. This gives a drawing very similar to a two point perspective, but it doesn't look quite right.

Oblique projections – see ◁**6**▷. The front surface is drawn flat on to the viewer, and the lines leading back from it are drawn at 45° to the horizontal.

   Oblique projections look rather odd too. To make them look more natural, draw the lines leading back from the front face half the length they should be according to the correct scale. But remember you have done this if you take measurements from the drawing.

Planometric projections – section 2.4 tells you about these.

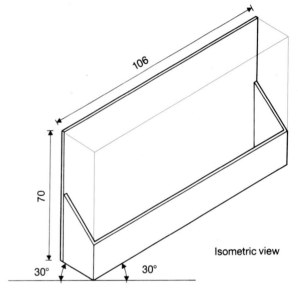

◁**5**▷ *In an **isometric projection**, parallel lines are drawn at 30° to the horizontal.*

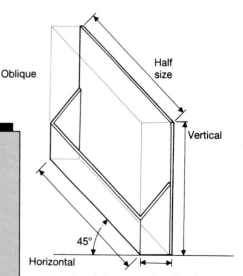

◁**6**▷ *An **oblique projection** has one face flat on. The lines leading back from it are drawn at 45° to the horizontal.*

---

1 Copy these symbols. Next to each one write down what it means.

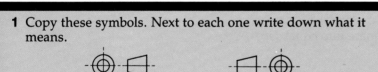

2 Draw an orthographic sketch of a small object, such as a Tic Tac sweet box. Use annotations to add all the information you can.

3 Name all the types of pictorial drawing mentioned in this section. Draw a 25 mm cube using each method. Annotate your cubes to explain the rules of each drawing method.

Drawing curves and circles

Do you need to draw it?

Drawing a curve accurately is harder than drawing a straight line. You can adjust the direction of a straight line until it looks right by **ghosting**. You can try drawing a curve by trial and error too, but it's much harder to do this. This section shows you some methods of drawing curves that 'look right'.

One way round the problem is to take a photograph. The film canister and coin in ◁1▷ both have curved edges. The photograph shows you their shape, colour and tone, and the familiar 50p piece shows the size of the canister. If this is what you want to show, a photograph is an ideal solution.

◁1▷ *A photograph can be a good way of showing a curved object. The coin shows you the size of the film canister.*

Drawing circles in 3 D images

◁2▷, ◁3▷ and ◁4▷ show you a method of drawing perspective views of circles quickly.

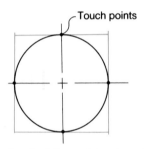

Touch points

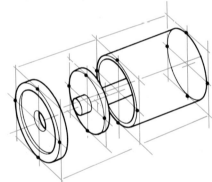

◁2▷ *Look at the points where this circle touches the square drawn around it.*

◁3▷ *Now imagine the square is the end of a guide box which could contain the film canister. The circle still touches the sides of the square at its mid-points.*

◁4▷ *Repeat the construction used in ◁3▷ several times to help you draw the canister inside the guide box.*

For larger curves use extra plot points

◁5▷, ◁6▷ and ◁7▷ show you how to mark off extra plot points for drawing larger circles. These points can be copied onto the ends of an enclosing box like the one in ◁3▷. A standard construction method has been used to divide the square into equal slices. You could do this with a ruler instead.

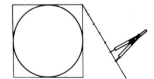

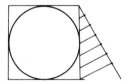

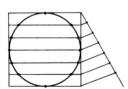

◁5▷ *Draw a line at an angle to one side of the square. Use compasses to make six equally spaced marks along the line.*

◁6▷ *Draw a line from the bottom mark to the edge of the square. Do the same for the other five marks. All these lines must be parallel.*

◁7▷ *Now draw parallel lines across the square like this. Mark where these lines cross the circle. These are your plot points.*

Circles in parallel pictorial projections

◁**8**▷ and ◁**9**▷ are **isometric** and **oblique projections** of the film canister. You can see how the plot points from ◁**7**▷ have been copied onto the ends of the guide boxes.

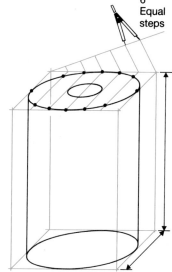

◁**8**▷ An **isometric projection** using the plot points taken from ◁**7**▷.

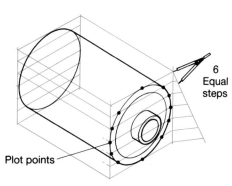

Use plot points to draw irregular curves

You can use plot points to draw a pictorial view of any curve. ◁**10**▷ is a first angle orthographic projection of a Stabilayout marker. The **end elevation** has been sliced to produce plot points on the curve. The plot points were used to produce the isometric projection of the cap in ◁**11**▷. Notice that the same slice lines were used to find plot points for the front and back curve of the cap.

Once you have mastered this technique you can use it to draw any shape in any parallel pictorial projection. You can use it to scale up, scale down, or do mirror images ◁**10**▷.

◁**9**▷ An **oblique** projection using the same 12 plot points.

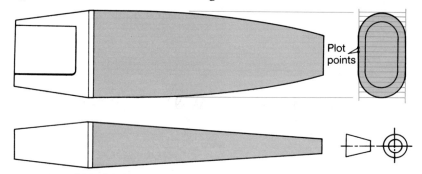

1ST ANGLE ORTHOGRAPHIC

◁**10**▷ Plot points from this **first angle orthographic projection** were used to make the drawing in ◁**11**▷.

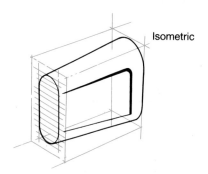

Isometric

◁**11**▷ An **isometric drawing** of the pen cap. The plot points come from the end elevation in ◁**10**▷.

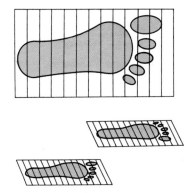

◁**12**▷ These footprints were made by using plot points to scale down the large picture, and by making mirror images of it.

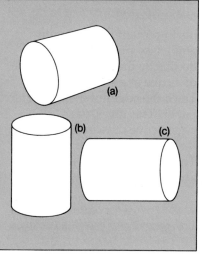

1 This cylinder represents a drink tin 40 mm long. Its diameter is 30 mm. Draw it:
 • with one circular end flat on
 • sitting on one circular end
 • on its side

2 Look at the instructions for finding plot points on page 28. Must all the slices be the same width? When might it be better for them to be different widths?

3 Draw some footsteps like those in ◁**12**▷.

Making accurate drawings

The further it gets, the smaller it looks

The further you get from an object, the smaller it *looks*. But you know that in reality it stays the same size. Equal sized parts of an object also look smaller if they are further away. Look at the way the studs on this LEGO battery holder appear to be larger at the front ◁**1**▷. This section shows you how to make details like this the right size in a drawing.

Start with an orthographic projection

Measure the holder and draw a formal **orthographic projection** of it. This will be an accurate visual record of the size and proportions of the holder ◁**2**▷.

Then add a grid

A square grid over the orthographic helps to show the location of each part of the holder. The grid in ◁**3**▷ divides the holder into six cubes. If you draw a perspective view of all these cubes joined together, you will have a guide box to draw the holder in.

Drawing cubes in perspective

It's important to make your guide box look right. You can do this by finding a photograph of a cube at a suitable angle. Trace the edges of the cube onto paper. This gives you a perspective drawing to use as the first cube in your guide box. This method is both easy and accurate.

◁**4**▷ *To make a perspective guide box, carefully trace off the first cube from a photograph. See ◁5▷*

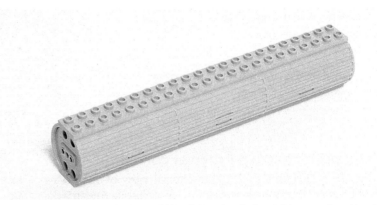

◁**1**▷ *A LEGO battery holder. With all the details it might seem hard to draw – but it isn't.*

◁**2**▷ *Start by drawing an accurate orthographic projection of the holder, showing its size, proportion and some details.*

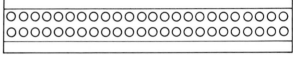
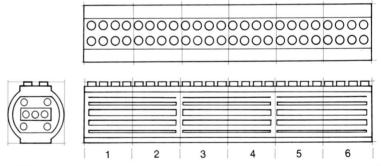

| 1 | 2 | 3 | 4 | 5 | 6 |

◁**3**▷ *Then draw a square grid over the holder. The holder is now enclosed by six boxes. It's easy to draw boxes in perspective.*

Making a guide box out of cubes

For the battery holder you will have to draw six cubes in a row. The cubes get smaller as they get closer to the vanishing points. ◁5▷ and ◁6▷ show you how to draw a second cube behind the one from ◁4▷. Repeat this process until you have six cubes in a row.

◁**5**▷ *Extend the top and bottom edges of your first cube towards the vanishing points. Find the middle of each vertical edge of the cube. Draw lines through these points towards the vanishing points.*

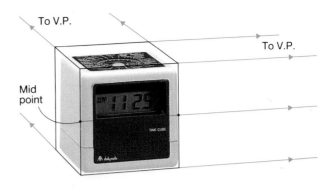

Using your perspective guide box

Each square on the grid in ◁3▷ matches a cube in your perspective guide box. You can draw each part of the holder the right size and in the right place by transferring the details from the grid to the guide box.

◁**6**▷ *Draw a straight line from A through B. Where it meets the bottom edge of the guide box at C, draw a vertical line to the top edge of the box at D. Now draw a line from D to the left-hand vanishing point. This completes the second cube.*

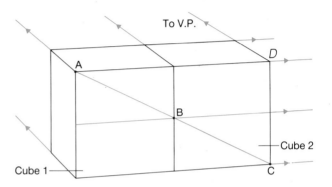

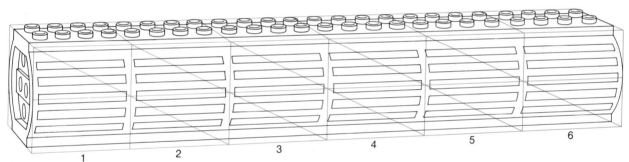

◁**7**▷ *The* **perspective guide box** *is used to get the proportions of the holder right. Then details are transferred into the box from* ◁**3**▷*.*

1 Use some photographs of cubes to make up some perspective guide boxes. You could start with the cubes in ◁4▷. Save these in your folder for future use.
2 Use copies of your perspective guide boxes to draw perspective views of:
  • the Toblerone packet in 2.1 ◁9▷
  • a spray can on its side

Looking inside an object

Why look inside?

You can't always discover what you want to know about an object just by looking at the outside. If you pick it up, the weight might give you an idea of what it is made from and whether it is hollow. If you tap it, the sound might give you more clues. This section suggests some ways to show the inside of the toy duck from 1.5.

◁**1**▷ Here is the toy duck from 1.5. This section shows several ways of showing what is inside it.

Exploding an object

When you show the inside of an object you must show the relationship between the parts and the whole object. If you don't, it will be hard for someone else to understand what you are showing them. One way of showing the inside is to imagine that the object has exploded apart, and the parts have been frozen in space, just far enough apart to let you see inside. Pictures like this are called **exploded views**.

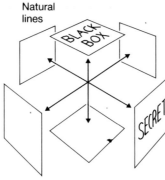

◁**2**▷ An **exploded view** of a cube. The sides have been exploded along **natural lines**.

Your exploded views will be clearest if you explode the parts apart along **natural lines**. In ◁2▷ this has been done to a hollow cube. There is more about natural lines in 2.1.

◁**3**▷ is an exploded view of the duck. First the head and top of the body were exploded along the vertical natural line. Next they were exploded apart along one of the horizontal lines. When it is difficult to see the way the object has been exploded, a thin line shows where things came from. You can see this on the duck's legs.

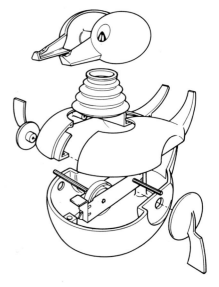

◁**3**▷ The duck has been exploded along two natural lines: upwards first, then outwards.

Looking through walls

Exploded diagrams aren't always suitable for complicated objects. It can be difficult to visualize the arrangement of the parts. Instead you could try using a **cut-away drawing**. ◁4▷ is drawn as if part of the front surface has been removed so that you can see inside the duck.

Sometimes you might find it better to draw the front surface to look transparent as in ◁5▷. This type of drawing gives you an impression of the whole object – the outside shape and the internal arrangement.

Inside orthographic drawings

You can show inside details in orthographic projections by drawing a **sectional elevation** like ◁6▷. This is what you would see if the duck had been sliced through and you were looking at the cut surface. Some parts of the drawing have hatch lines to tell you that the material has been sliced through. Different parts are hatched in different directions. This is a convention that tells you the parts are different. There is more about sections in 2.5.

Look at the cut-away and exploded views and see if you can identify the parts in the orthographic projection. The pictorial drawings give a better impression of the duck, but the orthographic gives much more accurate detail.

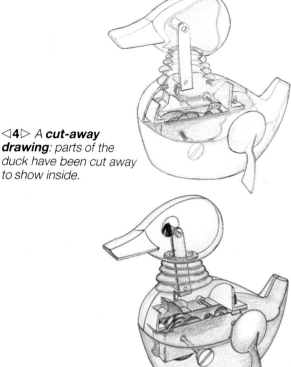

◁4▷ A **cut-away drawing**: parts of the duck have been cut away to show inside.

◁5▷ Here the front surface has been made transparent, but you can still see what the surface looks like.

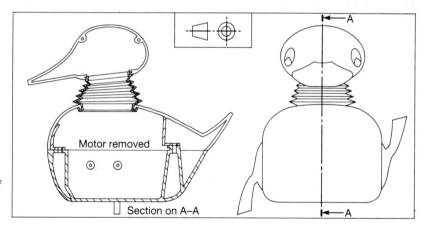

Motor removed

Section on A–A

◁6▷ A **section** shows the inside of the duck on this orthographic projection.

1 Use each of the three methods shown in this section to show a 24 mm diameter ball inside a 25 mm wide cardboard cube. Add annotations to explain the various parts and details shown in each drawing method.

2 The sectional elevation in ◁6▷ was taken on the centre line of the duck. Copy the drawing and colour it to show the parts that are sliced through and the parts that are not.

3 The exploded view in ◁3▷ was done along natural lines. Trace ◁3▷, but add pop-out eyes and a sailor's hat in their exploded positions.

How things fit together

Knock down articles

Many things you can buy are sold in kit form. They are called **knock down articles**. Manufacturers sell them in this form to save transportation and assembly costs. You need clear instructions to assemble articles of this type. Usually they come with an instruction booklet – a mixture of illustrations and notes. This section is about ways of showing how to assemble things.

LEGO kits

It is easy to make a model with LEGO. Most people know how it fits together and enjoy experimenting with the pieces. Also each kit includes simple instructions. **Sequential pictorial drawings** like ◁1▷ are used to take you step by step through the assembly. Look at the LEGO instructions and see how pictorial drawings are used to explain the assembly process.

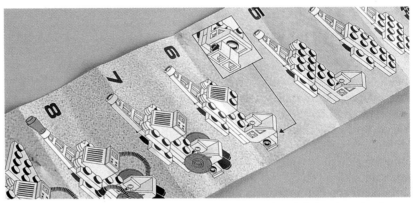

◁1▷ *LEGO instructions use pictorial drawings to show the assembly sequence.*

Assembling unfamiliar items

LEGO instructions assume that you will know and recognize LEGO parts. But the Zoids instructions in ◁2▷ show parts that are unique to this toy. The pictures show a lot of detail and the parts are labelled to help you recognize them. See how the arrows and notes help you along.

No matter how complicated the object is, assembly instructions can be clear and simple if they are well thought out.

① Left

Power Unit
②

Front side
①

② Right

③

③ Fix this gear before the other gear with boss is assembled.

Gear with boss

Gear

◁2▷ *This mixture of instructions, labels and drawings shows how a Zoids toy works.*

Instructions for permanent assembly

Assembly instructions must be very clear indeed if you have to put the object together correctly first time. ◁3▷ shows a kitchen unit which will be glued and screwed together permanently. Once you've started gluing you can't take the pieces apart.

Pictorial drawings would help here, but you would also need orthographic views to show exactly where parts like the screws go. Notes would help you cross-check in case you didn't understand the drawings. Good instruction booklets usually say the same thing in at least two different ways.

Remembering how things fit together

Sometimes you may need to dismantle an object to investigate something or to mend it. Use pictorial sketches like those in ◁4▷ to help you reassemble it correctly. If you are going to reassemble the object yourself, quick sketches will do. But if you want to show someone else what to do, your sketches will have to be more detailed.

Three techniques are used in ◁4▷

• an exploded (opened out) view of the thermostat is shown
• annotations label the parts and explain what to do
• numbers show the order in which things should be done

How much information should you show?

A skilled motor mechanic would not need the detail shown in ◁4▷ to assemble a thermostat. He would be able to recognize the parts and would not need the illustrations. A list like this would do:

> remove water outlet thermostat
> renew thermostat and gasket
> refit

The way you pass on information and the amount you give depend on who is going to use it. Unless you know otherwise it is best to assume that other people know very little.

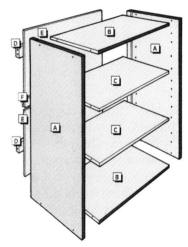

◁3▷ *These instructions show how to assemble a kitchen unit.*

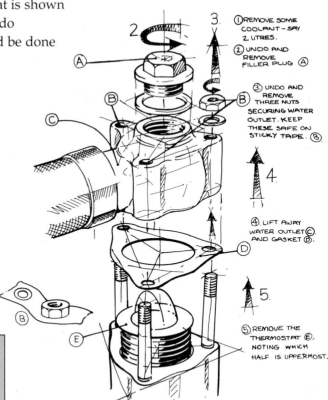

① REMOVE SOME COOLANT – SAY 2 LITRES.
② UNDO AND REMOVE FILLER PLUG Ⓐ
③ UNDO AND REMOVE THREE NUTS SECURING WATER OUTLET. KEEP THESE SAFE ON STICKY TAPE. Ⓑ
④ LIFT AWAY WATER OUTLET Ⓒ AND GASKET Ⓓ.
⑤ REMOVE THE THERMOSTAT Ⓔ, NOTING WHICH HALF IS UPPERMOST.

◁4▷ *These sketches and notes explain how to dismantle a car thermostat. Numbers show the order in which to do things.*

---

1 Take a pen apart. Sketch assembly instructions that another person could follow.
2 Design an instruction sheet to show how a pencil sharpener is:
   • assembled   • used
3 LEGO instructions come with very few words, but many pictures. Explain why.
4 Make a simple LEGO model, and design an assembly sheet for it.

Exercises on chapter 2

1 Toddler Toys is a company specializing in timber toys for children. They have decided they need a new cover picture for the boxes in which they sell their building block sets. The sets consist of wooden prisms and planks like those shown in ◁1▷.

- Draw a pictorial view of a toy which can be made from the building blocks and will appeal to young children. Use the drawing and the title 'Toddler Toys' in a design for the box cover.

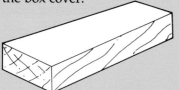 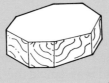 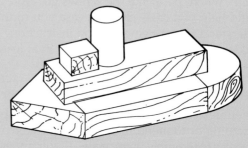

◁**1**▷ *Some of the Toddler Toys building blocks.*

2 Find a photograph of a house you like in a magazine. Trace its shape onto layout paper. Then design a double garage which could be built onto the side of the house and would be in keeping with the house design.

- Complete the picture as a pen and ink sketch. Add trees and bushes to show what the house will look like in a few years' time.
- Sketch elevations of your design on graph paper, showing both the house and garage.

3 Design a battery holder which can be used with LEGO kits. It should stack three HP11 batteries in a different way from the holder in 2.8. Your design must fit with existing LEGO pieces. Use a combination of drawing methods to explain your design.

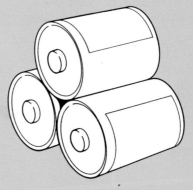

◁**2**▷ *Design a holder for three batteries.*

4 Design a quality pencil sharpener which would not look out of place on a company executive's desk. It must retain the pencil shavings. Use exploded views and cut-away diagrams to show your design, and how it would be emptied when full of shavings.

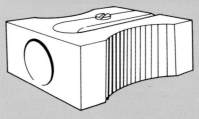

◁**3**▷ *Give me an executive image!*

5 Design a container which will hold six £1 coins, and will fit into a pocket. Use any method you like to show how coins are inserted and removed from the container.

Using colours and textures

Artists use colour to make their drawings look attractive. But designers use colour for other purposes such as indicating the shape of an object or making the details clearer. This chapter shows you how to make the best use of colour in your drawings.

Why use colour in drawings?

Colour helps you show ideas

When people say a drawing is colourful they usually mean that its colours make it look attractive. But designers use colour for many other purposes. When you are designing, you will use drawings to help you work out ideas and show them to other people. You must decide whether adding colour to your drawings will help in some way. Colour can be used to show the shape of an object, to draw attention to some part of it, or to make details clearer. This section shows several different reasons for using colour.

Using colour to show shape

Drawings can look very flat if they are not coloured or shaded. Compare the two drawings of a toy submarine in ◁2▷. Colour helps to show that the submarine's body is rounded. Because you know it is a submarine you might have guessed this anyway. But when you don't know what you are looking at, colouring or shading may be the only clue you have about an object's shape.

◁1▷ *This drawing by Leonardo da Vinci shows the shape of an armoured car **without** using colour.*

◁2▷ *Shading and colour stop this drawing of a toy submarine from looking flat.*

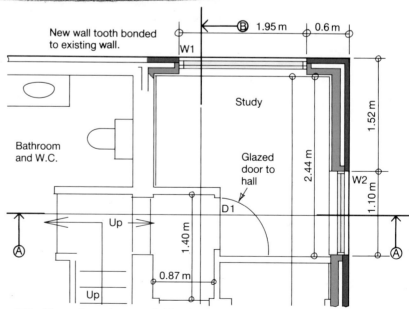

Colour draws attention to changes

◁3▷ shows an architect's plan for an extension to be built on the side of a house. This plan must be sent to the local council for planning permission before anything is built. The new rooms have been drawn on the plan in colour. This shows clearly which parts of the building are new, and draws the reader's eye to this part of the plan. Also, different colours have been used to show the different materials used in the extension: brickwork is shown in red, breeze blocks in green, and wood in yellow.

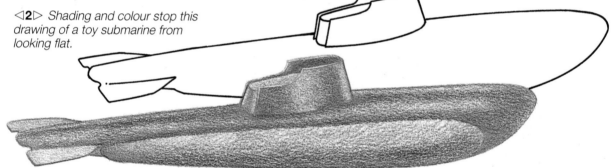

New wall tooth bonded to existing wall.

W1

Study

Bathroom and W.C.

Glazed door to hall

Up

Up

D1

W2

1.95 m   0.6 m

1.52 m

2.44 m

1.10 m

1.40 m

0.87 m

◁3▷ *The coloured parts of this plan draw your attention to an extension to the original building. (This building drawing uses different conventions from an engineering drawing.)*

Showing parts of a machine

◁4▷ was drawn by a student investigating a sewing machine mechanism. He has used colour to show the position of the part he is interested in – the mechanism that makes the needle move up and down. ◁5▷ shows a more complicated example of this technique. Different colours help you see the different systems that surround a very complicated device – the Joint European Torus experimental nuclear fusion reactor.

◁4▷ Here colour draws your attention to a mechanism in a sewing machine.

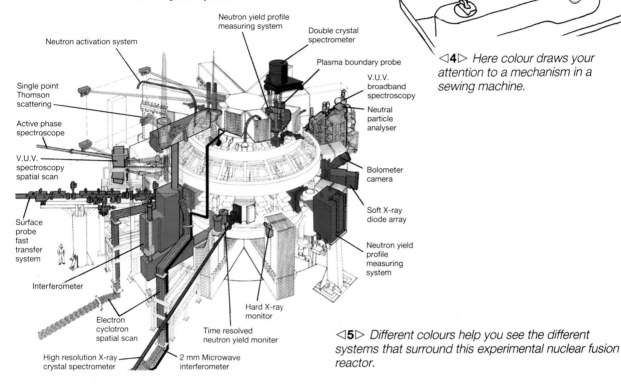

J.E.T. Diagnostic Systems

Neutron yield profile measuring system

Double crystal spectrometer

Neutron activation system

Plasma boundary probe

Single point Thomson scattering

V.U.V. broadband spectroscopy

Active phase spectroscope

Neutral particle analyser

V.U.V. spectroscopy spatial scan

Bolometer camera

Surface probe fast transfer system

Soft X-ray diode array

Interferometer

Neutron yield profile measuring system

Electron cyclotron spatial scan

Time resolved neutron yield moniter

Hard X-ray monitor

High resolution X-ray crystal spectrometer

2 mm Microwave interferometer

◁5▷ Different colours help you see the different systems that surround this experimental nuclear fusion reactor.

Cut through with colour

◁6▷ is a cut-away pictorial view into the mixer valve of a bathroom shower. Colour has been used to show where slices have been cut through different parts of the mixer. Slices through brass castings are coloured yellow, like the metal itself. Section 2.5 shows a way of drawing slices through surfaces using **hatching** instead. Nowadays most orthographic projections are drawn without using colour, but over 100 years ago, engineers such as Brunel used colour for orthographic projections of bridges, railways etc.

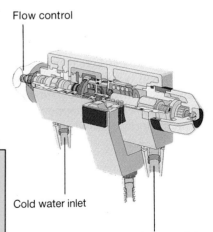

Flow control

Cold water inlet

Hot water inlet

◁6▷ Colour helps you see which parts of this shower mixer valve have been cut away to show its insides.

1 There are many different reasons for using colour in drawings. Write down as many reasons as you can think of.
2 Colour was not needed to show the shape of the armoured car in ◁1▷. Trace the outline of a submarine from ◁2▷ and try to show its shape without using colour.
3 Trace the outline of the sewing machine in ◁4▷. Then show the shape of the machine by colouring your drawing with a crayon or coloured pencil.
4 Use the technique shown in ◁6▷ to show the inside of a tomato. Colour and annotate your drawing.

Effective colouring techniques (I)

Easy ways to colour

When you are colouring drawings as part of your design work, use the quickest and easiest methods you can. You don't want to hold up your ideas by using difficult colouring techniques. The quickest method is **hatch shading** using the pen you are drawing with. Your sketch will only be one colour, but you can make darker **tones** by drawing over the shading lines several times. The computer disc box in ◁1▷ was drawn and hatch shaded with **fine line markers**. Different markers were used to increase the range of tones and colours.

Crayons add shade and texture

You can add colour to an ink sketch by using a coloured **crayon**. This is quick and it is easy to control where the colour goes. The effect will be better if you colour objects more darkly at their edges than in their middles.

If you place a **texture pad** under your drawing, the crayon will bring the texture through into your sketch ◁2▷. You can use all sorts of surfaces, from glasspaper to metal grilles, to obtain texture effects ◁3▷.

Mixing different media

Felt-tip markers, crayons, pencils and pens can all be used on the same drawing. Use thick markers for large areas of colour. Add details with pens, crayons and pencils – these media are easier to control when you are drawing details.

Pencils and crayons are made from different materials. Find out which ones will write over others. Some markers produce different colours on different types of paper. Others react together chemically. Always test your markers and pens together to see what happens *before* you use them on an important drawing.

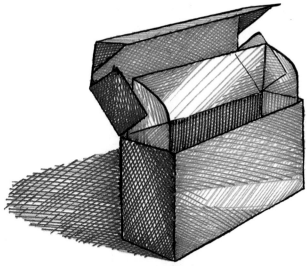

◁**1**▷ *Fine line markers were used to colour this pen and ink sketch and draw the shadow.*

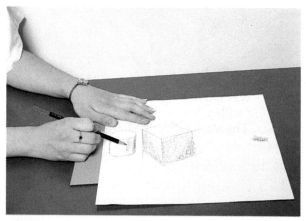

◁**2**▷ *To get a textured finish, place your drawing on a* **texture board** *and colour with crayons.*

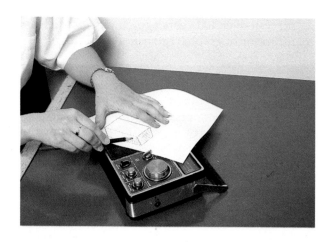

◁**3**▷ *Use surfaces like this radio grill to give your drawings texture. You can experiment with all sorts of textured surfaces to create interesting effects.*

Looking after your equipment

Try to build up a range of pens and markers for use in your design work. They last a long time, but even if they dry up they can sometimes be 'kept alive' by topping up with water or another **solvent** (chemical which dissolves the coloured pigment). Some media are water soluble (they dissolve in water), others are not. This can affect the way you use them. You must get to know your own equipment and the effects you can achieve.

Using backgrounds

◁4▷ is a charcoal rendered drawing of another disc box. The shadow behind the box acts as a background. It helps to draw attention to the picture *and* link it with the rest of the page. Without a background the drawing would look rather odd.

If you want to draw attention to a picture, don't draw too strong a background. A very strong background can *hide* a drawing. Another effective way of drawing backgrounds is shown in ◁5▷, and there is more about them in 3.4.

Shadows and highlights show shapes

Use shadows and highlights to help show the shapes of the objects you draw. The shadow in ◁1▷ was made by cross-hatching with a fine line marker. The tone of the shadow was darkened by drawing over the lines several times. You can get the same effect more quickly by using a darker marker.

Highlights are bright areas where light is reflected from the edges or corners of an object. ◁5▷ is a marker and crayon rendered drawing. White crayon highlights have been added. You can draw highlights with a white marker, crayon or pastel.

Gouache is good for highlighting. It is a strong paint which will cover most colours. If the base colour does bleed through the highlighting, use a fixative spray before you apply the white. There is more about fixatives in 3.5.

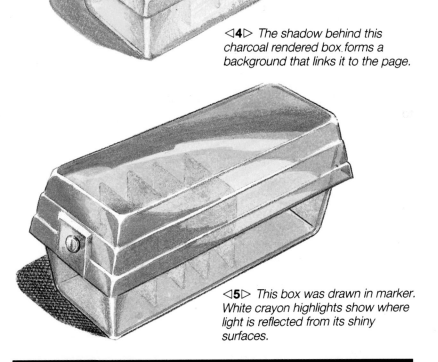

◁4▷ The shadow behind this charcoal rendered box forms a background that links it to the page.

◁5▷ This box was drawn in marker. White crayon highlights show where light is reflected from its shiny surfaces.

1 One reason for testing the colour of a marker is that the cap is not always the same colour as the ink. List some other reasons.
2 Look at the different methods of showing shadows used in ◁1▷, ◁4▷ and ◁5▷. Write brief notes to explain how each effect was achieved.
3 Trace the outline of a disc box from ◁4▷. Use crayons to colour the drawing. Make the sides of the box look rough not smooth.

Effective colouring techniques (II)

Experiment to avoid mistakes

Get your drawings looking right before you add any colour. If there are mistakes in your drawings, colouring won't hide them. If you want to experiment with a medium or colouring technique, try it out on a photocopy of your drawing first. See if the type of paper you want to draw on will work in your photocopier. This way you can get a good idea of the final effect without spoiling the original drawing.

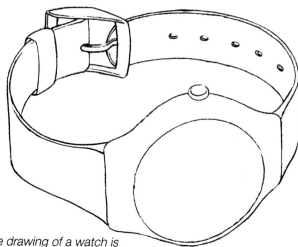

◁1▷ *This accurate drawing of a watch is ready for colour rendering. To avoid spoiling your drawings, practise colouring on photocopies first.*

Masks help you colour accurately

You may find it difficult to colour accurately up to an edge with a thick marker or a pastel wipe. Try using a **mask** – a protective cover which stops the colour getting to parts of your drawing where it is not wanted. You can make your own masks from materials such as paper and plastic. Paper masks work well when you are rendering with crayon or pastel. Plastic masks work well with markers.

How to use and re-use masking film

The pictures below show you how to use **masking film** – a sticky plastic film which comes on a shiny backing sheet. The film can be peeled off your drawing after use. This is an expensive but very accurate way to mask.

You can use masking film to render with several different colours side by side. After using a mask for one colour, save it on the backing sheet until the ink is dry. Then you can re-use it with another colour.

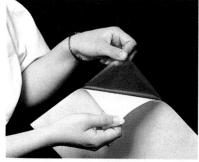

◁2▷ ***Masking film*** *comes on a protective backing sheet. Save used film on the backing sheet for re-use.*

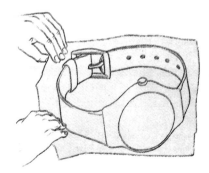

◁3▷ *Cover the part of the drawing you want to mask with a sheet of plastic masking film.*

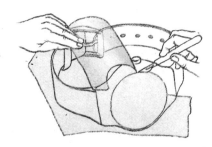

◁4▷ *Using a sharp blade, carefully cut the film away from the area to be coloured.*

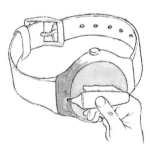

◁5▷ *Colour in the exposed area. When using a marker, cover the area with wide strips of colour.*

Rendering with pastel and talc

When you render with pastel on smooth paper you can get sharp edges without using a mask. You can do this by using a **plastic eraser** to rub away areas of pastel. The trick is to fill in the grain of the paper with talcum powder *before* you use the pastel. This prevents the pastel from getting deep into the paper, so none will be left there when you rub it away with the eraser. You can also use the eraser to show highlights as shown in ◁6▷.

The best way to apply pastel smoothly is to powder it and brush it on with a cotton wool pad. Section 3.4 shows you how. If you do use powdered pastel, it should be **fixed** with a clear plastic fixative spray. This sticks the powder to the paper and prevents any smudging.

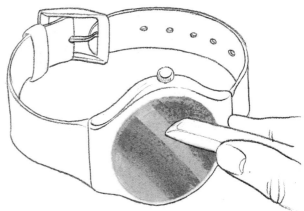

◁6▷ *This watch face has been rendered in pastel. Highlights are being 'cut away' with a plastic eraser.*

Special effects with pastels, crayons and markers

◁7▷ and ◁8▷ show two different ways of rendering the same drawing of a watch.

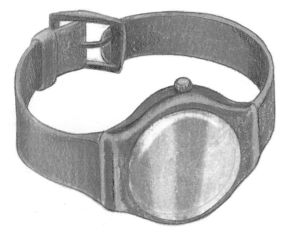

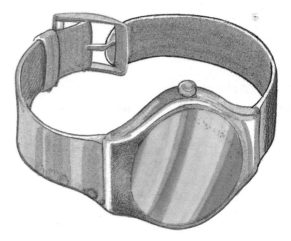

◁7▷ *This watch has been fully rendered in pastel and crayon. The clear plastic over the watch face has been shown by cutting through the pastel with a plastic eraser.*

Pastel is a soft medium, so hard edges were added with a crayon. Light crayon was used for highlights and dark crayon for edges in shadow.

◁8▷ *Here is the same watch rendered with markers. Crayons and fine line markers were used to add sharp details.*

This time the clear plastic effect was achieved by sticking tracing paper to the drawing. Dark areas of tracing paper are marked on both sides. Pale areas are only marked on the front.

---

1 Masking film is cut away with a sharp blade. Think of a way of cutting accurate masks without cutting into your drawings.
2 Trace the watch from ◁1▷. Cut masks to help you render:
   - a pale background behind the watch
   - a dark strap
   - a light watch face
3 Use the technique shown in ◁7▷ to draw a coffee table with a glass top.

Filling in the background

Why use backgrounds?

Coloured backgrounds can draw attention to a drawing or photograph and link it to words or other pictures on a page. A rendered drawing can look rather odd on a plain white page without a background. Section 3.2 ◁4▷ and ◁5▷ show two ways of adding background colouring to a drawing. The simplest way is to draw on coloured paper. This section shows you some other techniques.

These pictures of a roller skate, ◁1▷ to ◁3▷, have been cut out and stuck onto pre-prepared backgrounds. It is quicker to get clean edges this way than it is to use masks.

◁1▷ *This background was made by wiping dry pastel across a smooth sheet of paper. Then the paper was cut carefully at an angle. The two pieces were pasted down with the roller skate drawing onto another sheet of paper of a complementary colour.*

◁2▷ *Here is another dry pastel background. A border has been drawn around the pastel with a wide marker. The border and the pastel are **complementary colours** so they go well together.*

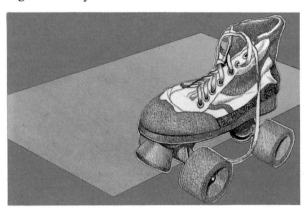

◁3▷ *This background was produced by masking areas of a coloured and textured paper. Then a wide marker was drawn across the paper to produce the stripes. Remember to test for colour changes when using markers on coloured papers.*

Pastel backgrounds

Two dry pastel backgrounds are shown on the opposite page. Pastel can also be used to make bold striped backgrounds like the one in ◁4▷. This is done by wiping wet pastel across the paper.

◁4▷ *Here the roller skate drawing has been glued to a background made by wiping wet pastel across the paper. The background has been* **fixed** *so that the glue will stick to its surface.*

How to make a wet pastel background

Pictures ◁5▷ to ◁9▷ show you how to make a pastel background like the one in ◁4▷.

Similar effects can be achieved by using coloured inks on cotton wool or felt, or by applying powdered **Stabilo Carb-Othello** with wet cotton wool. Invent your own ways of producing backgrounds. Here are some ideas:

● try different sprays on wet and dry surfaces
● try mixing oil-based and water-based colours

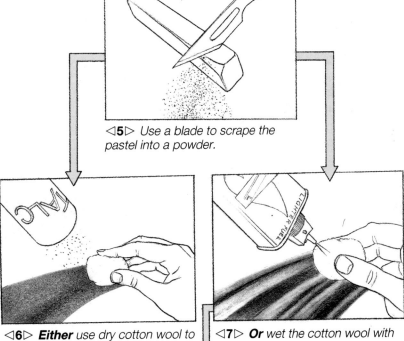

◁5▷ *Use a blade to scrape the pastel into a powder.*

◁6▷ **Either** *use dry cotton wool to apply the pastel dust smoothly . . .*

◁7▷ **Or** *wet the cotton wool with Cleanart fluid before you apply the pastel dust. This gives a banded effect.*

1 Draw a two-point perspective of an object in the design studio. Mount it against one of your favourite backgrounds.
2 Make an information poster showing other people how to achieve some of the background effects shown in this section. Add some effects of your own.

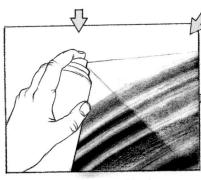

◁8▷ *When the pastel is dry, use a* **fixative spray** *to stop it smudging.*

◁9▷ *Paste your rendered drawing onto the pastel background.*

Sprays in the studio

Why use sprays?

Spraying is a very effective way of putting a thin layer of colour, fixative or glue onto a surface. You can achieve an even cover that is not possible with any other method. The quality of the results makes the extra time and effort involved worthwhile.

Spray is difficult to control. Particles of glue or ink will float onto parts of a drawing where you don't want it unless you use a **mask**. Section 3.3 shows how to use masks.

Spray healthy

Sprays can cause health hazards so you should take great care to use them properly. If you use a spray in an unventilated area you will breathe in particles of glue or pigment mixed with solvent vapour. This can be harmful, especially when you are using glues and fixatives, so **follow this health warning**:

- **do your spraying outside, or in a bay with an air extractor**

If this isn't possible then:

- **use a face mask, or don't use the spray**

Simple ways of spraying

Here are two simple ways of spraying ink or paint:

◁**1**▷ *A wide variety of spray equipment is used in the design studio to apply even layers of colour, fixative or glue.*

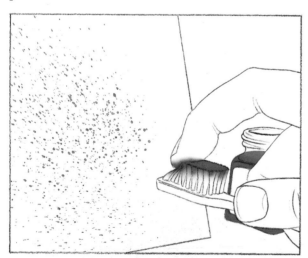

◁**2**▷ **Spatter spraying** – *this works with most types of ink or paint. Pull back the toothbrush bristles, then release them, spattering the ink over your drawing. You don't have precise control over where the spray goes, but the results are effective.*

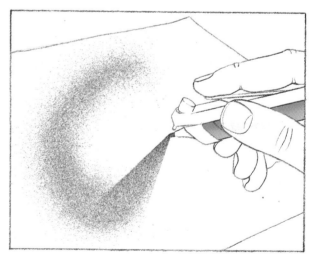

◁**3**▷ **Spraying marker ink** – *if you blow air across the tip of a marker, drops of ink will be blown onto your drawing. Use compressed air from an airbrush, or a* **Letrajet** *like the one shown here.*

Airbrushes offer more control

An airbrush is a spray gun which uses a jet of air to propel small droplets of ink. The airbrush is connected to a compressor which provides a constant supply of fast moving air.

Airbrushes are used to render very high quality drawings like ◁**4**▷. They can produce results that look as convincing as photographs. Airbrushes come in two main types – single and double action.

How to use airbrushes

You will need to practise a lot if you want to be good at airbrushing. Here are some basic rules to follow:

- start with a *clean* airbrush
- use good quality paper and masking film, and have a sharp blade handy to cut the mask
- plan ahead by colouring a *copy* of your drawing with crayon first, so you know how you will colour each part
- practise airbrushing on copies of your drawings first
- don't be afraid to use crayons to 'finish' your drawing
- don't start if you are in a hurry!

A simple airbrush technique

Not all airbrushing is complicated. ◁**6**▷ shows you how to use a paper mask to produce a cloud effect. This would make a good background for a drawing. If you experiment you will discover simple techniques like this yourself. When you see someone else using a good trick, don't be afraid to try it out.

1 Make a chart listing the advantages and disadvantages of using sprays.
2 What safety precautions should you take with all spraying techniques? Look at section 5.4, then make a chart showing how to use sprays safely.
3 What type of spray would be used to do each of these jobs – give a reason with each answer:
   - fixing a pastel drawing
   - drawing a 'photographic' image for an advertisement
   - painting the case of a model flashgun

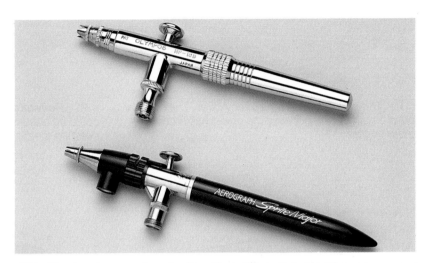

◁**4**▷ *This high quality artwork was produced using a double action airbrush like the one in* ◁**5**▷.

◁**5**▷ *The top, inexpensive* **single action airbrush,** *is ideal for backgrounds and models which do not need fine detail. Single action means the air and ink are mixed automatically and cannot be controlled separately. The bottom, more expensive,* **double action airbrush** *lets you control the ink and air supply separately. It is much more precise and it can be used for fine detailed artwork.*

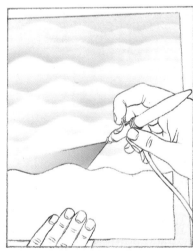

◁**6**▷ *Airbrushing a* **cloud effect** *– move a wavy paper mask down the page as you spray. Let the mask rest for longer in some places than in others.*

Showing what it's made of

Giving visual clues

You can give visual clues in your drawings to show what an object is made of. There are many ways of doing this. You can use colour, shape, texture to give clues. This section shows some methods you can use.

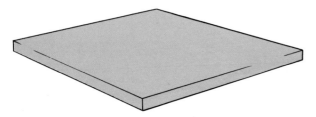

◁**1**▷ *This picture doesn't give many clues. The material looks hard, but only because the object has straight, sharp edges.*

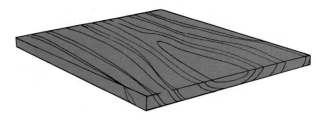

◁**2**▷ **Reflection lines** *make this material look shiny. It could be opaque glass (non see-through), plastic, or polished metal.*

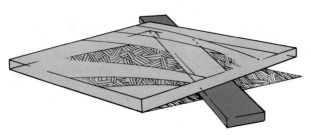

◁**3**▷ *You can see through this material so it isn't metal. It's propped up on a bar but it isn't bent, so it must be rigid. It could be either plastic or glass.*

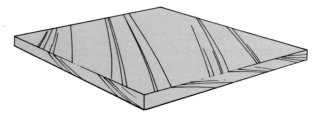

◁**4**▷ *This material is obviously wood. A good clue is given by the wood grain which has been drawn on the top surface and the sides of the block.*

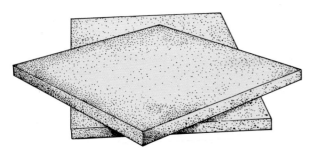

◁**5**▷ *The texture shows that this material could be either sand or concrete. There's another clue: the top block is hanging over an edge without breaking. So which material do you think it's made of?*

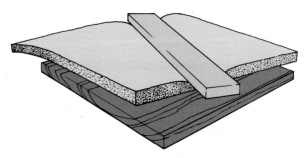

◁**6**▷ *You can almost be certain this is flexible foam. The sagging corner and compressed edge wouldn't occur in concrete or sand. No clues show what the bar is made of, but the compression of the foam tells you that it's heavy.*

Different types of reflections

If you can see sharp reflections in a surface, the material must have a smooth mirror-like finish. A diffuse reflection (in which the reflected object looks dull and spread out) means the material has a smooth but dull finish. It could be painted matt or made from slightly 'frosted' plastic.

<7> *The sharp reflection and accurate colours suggest a mirror or a chrome plated surface.*

<8> *This dull reflection suggests the mirroring material has a smooth but dull finish.*

Some shapes give clues . . .

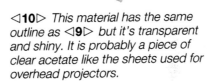

<9> *Here the outline suggests a thin floppy material, but it could be something **hard** and **curved**. It's not transparent and it doesn't reflect things – it could be card or paper.*

<10> *This material has the same outline as <9> but it's transparent and shiny. It is probably a piece of clear acetate like the sheets used for overhead projectors.*

<11> *Sharp bends show that these sheets are more rigid than the materials in <9> and <10>. The colour and thickness give more clues. One is metal, the other plastic – which is which?*

. . . other shapes don't

Sometimes you can't use the shape of an object to help show what material it's made from. Then you have to use colour and texture to suggest what the material is. Try matching the colours and textures in the pictures below to the descriptions in the caption.

a   b   c   d   e

<12> *Match the drawings to these descriptions:*

- *cotton wool* • *oil puddle*
- *pile of sand*
- *outline on paper.*
- *hole in the ground*

The outlines all give you the same message – the colours and textures give you the clues.

1 Some colours suggest particular materials. Make a checklist showing which colours you associate with different materials.
2 Make a list of materials which would show reflections. Write notes on the types of reflections you would see in each material – would they be sharp or diffuse?
3 Trace the outlines of the shapes in <12> and see if you can use colour and texture to make them suggest other materials. (For example – if you added small trees to <a> it could be a mountain.)

Extra help for the designer

Why use new technology?

If you have access to new technology that can make designing easier, use it! You can use mechanical, electronic and photographic aids to help work out and show your designs. This isn't cheating. Your design ideas are more important than the methods you use to develop or show them. This section shows some techniques you may find useful.

Photocopiers have many uses

A **photocopier** is invaluable in a school design studio. Here are just a few of the things you can do with one:

- make several copies of an original drawing, then experiment with different colour rendering techniques
- cut up drawings, paste them in new positions, then photocopy them to get a new original
- reproduce your own logo on each sheet of a project to show that the sheets are linked to one another
- copy photographs, then colour them with markers
- enlarge or reduce drawings.

◁1▷ **Photocopiers** can be used to achieve some stunning effects. Some small circulation magazines and fanzines are run off on photocopiers.

Word processing

A microcomputer with a word processing option is very useful. You can use it to annotate your drawings, and to arrange text to fit into the space you have available. Try using different **fonts** – styles and sizes of letters. Print a **hard copy** of your text on paper, then cut it out and paste it onto your drawing. This is a quick and professional-looking way of labelling your drawings. And if you have a spelling checker in your word processor, you have no excuse for mistakes!

◁2▷ **Word processors** allow you to adjust the size and shape of your text to fit available space, and print it out neatly.

Cut and paste to lay out pages

Cut and paste just means cutting out text and illustrations and sticking them down on another sheet of paper. It's a way of getting the right drawings and text next to one another on a page. This book went through a cut and paste stage.

After pasting your text and drawings down, make a photocopy to get your finished page. If you can see dark shadow lines on the photocopy around each piece of text or drawing, try:

- adjusting the photocopier to make lighter copies
- using typewriter correcting fluid on the edge of each piece of text or drawing before copying
- working on thinner paper

◁3▷ **Cut and paste** – the text and illustrations of part of this book are being pasted down onto a grid. Photographs will be added at a later stage.

Drawing using cameras . . .

Cameras can help you make accurate drawings. Take a picture of the view you want and have it made into a slide. Then you can project the image onto paper and trace around the shape. A slide projector will let you adjust the picture to the size you want.

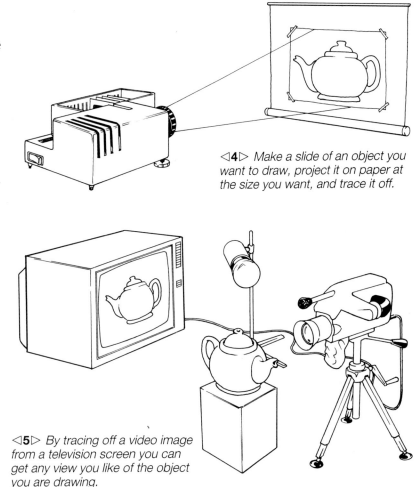

◁**4**▷ *Make a slide of an object you want to draw, project it on paper at the size you want, and trace it off.*

. . . and video cameras

You can get an image of an object on a television screen by using a **video camera** and a spotlight. Change the size and angle until you have the picture you want, then trace the image onto layout paper taped to the screen. This is a good way of getting the shadows in your drawings right. You can also find the positions of highlights by adjusting the contrast on the video camera.

◁**5**▷ *By tracing off a video image from a television screen you can get any view you like of the object you are drawing.*

Printing pictures from a video camera

With the aid of a **digitizer** it is possible to pass a picture from a video camera into a microcomputer and display it on a computer screen. Then the image on the screen can be printed using either a **dot matrix printer** or a **laser printer**.

Some computer's programs allow you to alter images while they are on the screen. You can change colours, stretch the image, and erase or add details before printing it.

◁**6**▷ *A video image of the airship gondola was passed through a **digitizer** into a **microcomputer**, then printed out on a **dot matrix printer**.*

1 Make a list of ways in which a designer could make use of a photocopier. Include some new ideas of your own.
2 Three ways of recording images of 3D objects are shown on this page. How would you rate each method for speed and accuracy? Discuss your ideas with a friend then make notes on your conclusions.
3 Photocopiers and laser printers don't use ink. Find out what they do use and why it has this name. (Clue: it begins with T).

Exercises on chapter 3

1 Imagine you are a designer for an 'up market' trophy manufacturer. You have been asked to design new trophies for dominoes, draughts and chess tournaments.
   - The trophies must be simple to make, and made of good quality materials.
   - Produce a presentation drawing for one of the trophies. It should be clear from the drawing what types of materials the trophy will be made from.

2 Design a poster for the design studio to show the precautions that should be taken when spray equipment is used. Section 3.5 will help.
   - Include details of dangers related to specific sprays. These are usually printed on the sides of spray cans.
   - The poster should be eye-catching from a distance, but the safety details should hold the reader's attention too.

3 Design a bubble pack in which a toothbrush can be sold. Keep your design as simple as possible.
   - Draw the pack showing the brush *inside* the plastic bubble.
   - Use any colouring method you like to show the transparency of the plastic.

4 The Russian doll ◁3▷ has four other dolls inside the outer one, each a little smaller than the one before.
   - Use any two methods of your choice to show that this is more than one doll.

5 Produce a range of different backgrounds that can be used with your design drawings. Keep them in a folder with notes explaining how you produced each one. Add new backgrounds to your folder as you discover new techniques.

◁1▷ See if you can improve on the design of these sports trophies.

◁2▷ A typical toothbrush bubble pack. Can you improve the design?

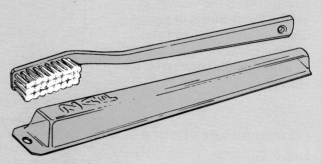

◁3▷ Find two ways of showing that this Russian doll has four smaller dolls inside it.

Useful geometry and constructions

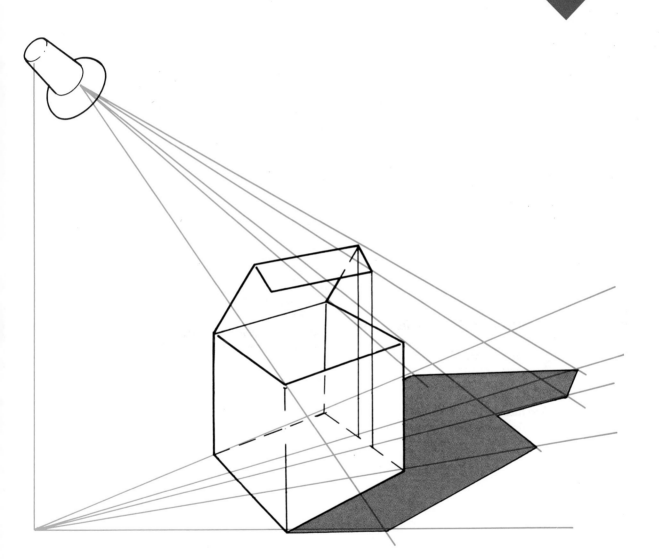

You can use geometry to help you draw shadows and to draw certain shapes
quickly and accurately. This chapter shows you how.

Some useful geometry

Geometrical constructions

This section shows you some useful **geometrical constructions** – ways of drawing certain shapes, and dividing lines or angles into equal parts. Only use constructions if they will help you work more quickly or accurately than another method.

Dividing a line into equal parts

◁**1**▷ and ◁**2**▷ show you how to divide a line into *two* equal parts using compasses. This construction also gives you the **perpendicular bisector** – a line at right angles to your original line that cuts it in two.

◁**3**▷ to ◁**5**▷ show you how to divide a line into *three* equal parts using compasses, a set square and a ruler. You can use the same method to divide a line into *any* number of equal parts.

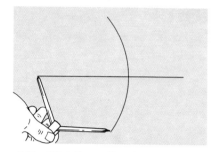

◁**1**▷ **Dividing a line into two equal parts** – Set your compasses to more than half the length of the line you want to divide in two. Put the point on one end of the line. Then draw a wide arc cutting through the line.

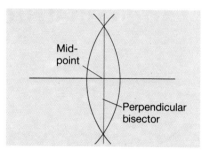

◁**2**▷ Without adjusting the compasses, move the point to the other end of the line and draw another arc. Draw a straight line to connect the points where the arcs cut each other. This line is the perpendicular bisector.

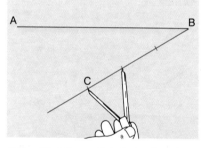

◁**3**▷ **Dividing a line into three equal parts** – Draw a new line at an angle to the first one. Use your compasses to make three equally spaced marks along the new line. Here the final mark is labelled C.

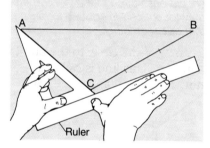

◁**4**▷ Use the long edges of a set square to draw a line connecting A to C. Then hold the set square steady in the same position and move a ruler against its bottom edge. Hold the ruler steady.

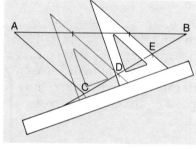

◁**5**▷ Move the set square along the ruler to the next mark – D. Then make a mark where the set square crosses AB. Repeat this for each mark on line CB. The marks on AB divide it into three equal parts.

Dividing an angle into equal parts

◁**6**▷ and ◁**7**▷ show you how to divide an angle into two equal parts using compasses.

◁**6**▷ **Dividing an angle into two equal parts** – First use compasses to draw an arc across the angle. Here the ends of the arc are marked A and B. Don't adjust the compasses.

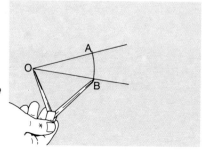

◁**7**▷ Move the compasses and draw two more arcs from the points A and B. Then draw a line from O to the point where the new arcs cross. This line divides the angle in half.

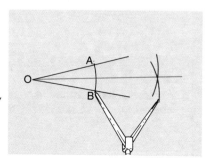

Constructing angles

◁8▷ shows you how to use compasses to draw an **equilateral triangle** – a triangle with all sides the same length and all angles equal to 60°. The equilateral triangle is a strong shape often used by designers in packaging and other structures.

The construction in ◁8▷ can be used to make other angles such as 120°, 90°, 45°, and 30° by starting with 60° and adding and dividing angles.

Drawing circles that touch or cut

When you draw circles or **arcs** (parts of circles) *touching* one another, follow this rule to make your drawing look right:

▷ A straight line drawn between the centres of the two circles should pass through the point where the circles touch. ◁

Don't follow this rule for circles or arcs that *cut* each other.

Drawing tangents

A **tangent** is a straight line touching the edge of a circle. The point where the line touches the circle is the **point of tangency**. A line drawn from the centre of the circle to the point of tangency is at right angles to the tangent. This line is called a **normal**. ◁11▷ to ◁13▷ show you how to draw a tangent at any point on the edge of a circle.

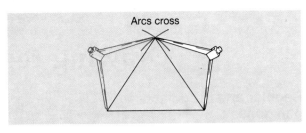

◁8▷ **Constructing an equilateral triangle** – Draw one side of the triangle. Set the compasses to the same length as this side. Then draw arcs from points A and B. Where the arcs cross is the third point of the triangle.

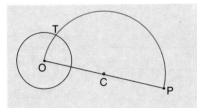

◁9▷ When arcs or circles **touch**, a straight line between their centres should pass through the point where they touch. This is not true for arcs that **cut** each other.

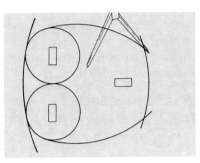

◁10▷ In this design for a 13 amp plug, which curves touch and which curves cut?

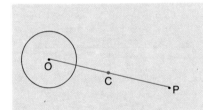

◁11▷ **Finding the tangent to a circle from any point P** – Draw a line from O to P. Find and mark its centre C.

◁12▷ Set your compasses to length CP. Draw a semi-circle from point C. It crosses the original circle at point T.

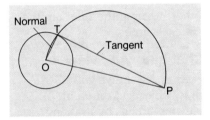

◁13▷ Draw a triangle by joining the points O P and T. The line PT is the **tangent**. OT is the **normal**.

1 Draw a straight line, then divide it into three equal parts using the method shown in ◁3▷. Do you need a ruler, or would any straight edge do?

2 Look at the touching curves in ◁9▷. If you draw a tangent to one of the curves at the point where they touch, will it be a tangent to the other curve too? Explain your answer.

3 Use compasses to construct an equilateral triangle. Then construct the following angles by starting with a 60° angle and adding and dividing angles: 120° 90° 45° 30°

Drawing regular shapes

Regular and irregular polygons

Regular geometrical shapes like ◁**1**▷ and ◁**2**▷ are often used by designers working on packaging and company logo design. These shapes are **regular polygons** – each side is straight *and* the same length. Also, the angles between the sides are the same. **Irregular polygons** have straight sides which aren't all the same length, and the angles between the sides differ too.

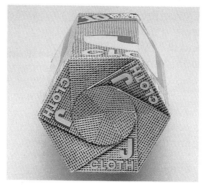

◁**1**▷ *The end of this J Cloth box is based on a* **hexagon** *– a six-sided regular polygon.*

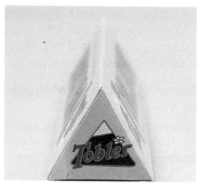

◁**2**▷ *The end of this Toblerone packet is based on an* **equilateral triangle**.

What's your angle?

Here is a useful fact to help you draw regular polygons:

▷ You can find the angles marked A in these pictures by dividing 360° by the number of sides the polygon has. ◁

For an **octagon** (an eight sided polygon) the angle A is 360° ÷ 8 = 45°. So you can draw an octagon by drawing eight sides the same length, one after the other, turning the ruler another 45° each time.

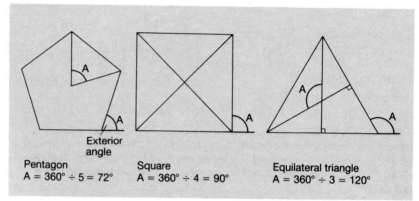

Pentagon
A = 360° ÷ 5 = 72°

Square
A = 360° ÷ 4 = 90°

Equilateral triangle
A = 360° ÷ 3 = 120°

Exterior angle

◁**3**▷ *For any regular polygon, the angles marked A can be found by dividing 360° by the number of sides the polygon has.*

Changing your view

Section 2.1 shows you how to draw objects at different viewing angles by drawing guide boxes around them. You can do this with polygons too. ◁**4**▷ and ◁**5**▷ show you how to draw a polygon at any viewing angle. This would help you make an accurate drawing of the prisms in Section 2.1.

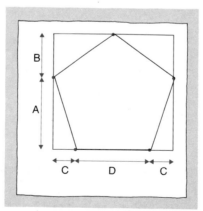

◁**4**▷ ***Drawing a polygon at any angle*** *– Draw a guide box around the polygon. Mark where it touches the sides of the box. Notice the position of each touch point – is it half way along the side? a third of the way?*

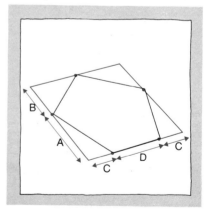

◁**5**▷ *Now draw the guide box at the viewing angle you want. Mark in the points where the polygon would touch it. Remember how far along each side they are. Join them together to get your polygon.*

Special constructions

Here are three special methods of drawing some polygons quickly in particular situations. They are not universal – they don't work for all polygons.

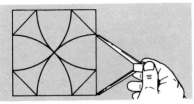

◁6▷ **An octagon inside a square** – Set the compasses to half the square's diagonal. Draw arcs in the square from each corner. Join the points where the arcs touch the square.

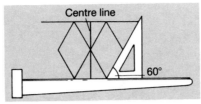

◁7▷ **Drawing a hexagon between two pre-set lines** –First draw a centre line. Then use the 60° angle of a set square to draw these lines.

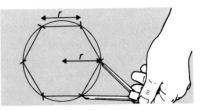

◁8▷ **A hexagon inside a circle** – The length of each side is equal to the radius of the circle. Set your compasses to this length and mark the sides off around the circle.

Fitting a polygon into a circle

◁9▷ to ◁11▷ show you how to draw a polygon to fit exactly into a circle. This is a **universal construction** – it will work for all polygons.

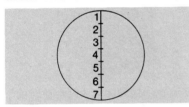

◁9▷ **Drawing a heptagon (seven sides) inside a circle** – Draw a diameter across the circle and divide it into 7 equal parts. Here they are numbered.

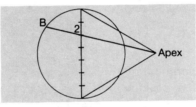

◁10▷ Then draw an equilateral triangle on the diameter. Draw a line from the triangle's apex, through point 2, to meet the edge of the circle at B.

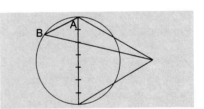

◁11▷ Join A to B. AB is one side of the polygon. Set your compasses to this length, AB, and mark off the other sides around the circle.

Using circles to help draw polygons

◁12▷ to ◁14▷ show a way of constructing a polygon when you know how long you want each side to be. This is done by drawing the circle the polygon would fit into, and marking off the sides around the circle. This is another universal construction . . . or is it?

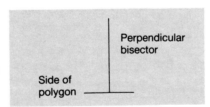

◁12▷ Draw one side of the polygon to the length you have chosen. Then draw its perpendicular bisector (details in 4.1 ◁2▷).

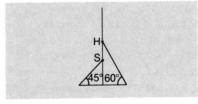

◁13▷ Draw lines from the ends of the side to the bisector at the angles shown. Points **S** and **H** would be the centres of circles around a **S**quare and **H**exagon.

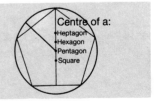

◁14▷ **P** (halfway between **S** and **H**) is the centre of a circle round a **P**entagon. Add equally spaced marks above **S** to find the centres of circles round other polygons.

1 There is a special relationship between equilateral triangles and hexagons. Draw a picture to show how they are related.
2 The shape of a 50p coin is based on a regular heptagon but the sides are curves. Find out where the centres of these curves would be. Then draw a 50p coin at twice the real size.
3 Try drawing polygons using the method shown in ◁12▷ to ◁14▷. Find the polygon with the largest number of sides you can draw accurately. Is this construction method truly universal (will it work for any polygon)?

Surface developments

What is a surface development?

A **surface development** shows the shape of a
sheet of material from which a three-dimensional
object can be formed. The sheet can be bent or
folded to make the object but it cannot be
stretched or compressed. This section shows you
some useful surface developments.

For complicated objects like ◁**1**▷ you may need
to use several step-by-step sketches to show how
to get from the development ◁**2**▷ to the end
product.

In industry, surface developments are often
used to find out how much material is needed to
make a product. You can do this too when you
are making models or mock-ups of your designs
from card or plastic sheet. Then you will know
the size and shape of sheet needed.

Developing a cube

◁**3**▷ to ◁**5**▷ show the surface development of a
cube. If you were designing a 'fold-flat' packing
box you could use pictorial sketches like these to
show how to make it up.

Developing a pyramid

◁**8**▷ shows the development of
a pyramid which has a square
base. In an elevation or 'end-on'
view of a pyramid the sides
slope away from you and the
line Ax appears shorter than it
really is. So you can't measure
Ax straight off the elevation. Instead you need to
find the true length AX before you draw a
development. ◁**7**▷ shows you how.

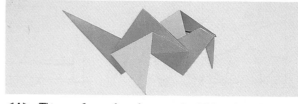

◁**1**▷ *The* **surface development** *of this origami bird is
the flat sheet shown in* ◁**2**▷.

◁**2**▷ *About twelve step-by-step sketches are needed
to show how to fold this development to make the bird
in* ◁**1**▷.

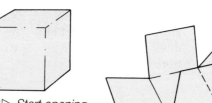

◁**3**▷ *Start opening
the cube . . .*

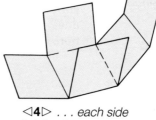

◁**4**▷ *. . . each side
is joined to at
least one other . . .*

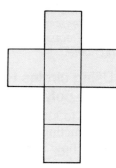

◁**5**▷ *. . . the surface
development is flat.*

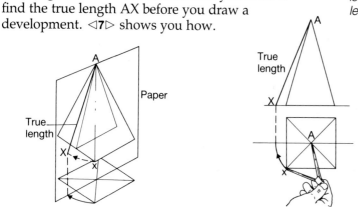

◁**6**▷ *In an elevation of a pyramid,
some sides look shorter. You can
find the true lengths by* **turning** *the*
pyramid.

◁**7**▷ *Use dividers to find the new
position of the corner x when the
base is turned. Then measure the
true length XA.*

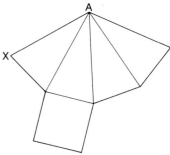

◁**8**▷ *This development of the
pyramid was made using the true
length XA.*

Developing a cylinder

◁**9**▷ to ◁**11**▷ shows the development of a cylinder. The rectangle ◁**11**▷ has sides which are the height and circumference of the cylinder.

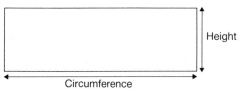

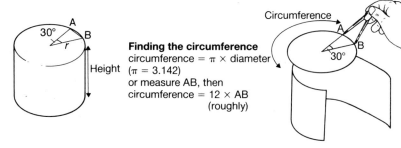

Finding the circumference
circumference = π × diameter
(π = 3.142)
or measure AB, then
circumference = 12 × AB
(roughly)

◁**9**▷ *Developing a cylinder . . .*   ◁**10**▷ *. . . it unfolds . . .*

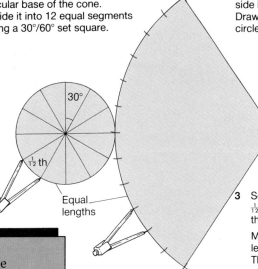

◁**11**▷ *. . . into a rectangle and two circles.*

◁**12**▷ *Two elevations of a cone. On one of the views the line XY is a true length – Which one?*

Developing a cone

◁**13**▷ shows you how to draw the development of a cone. You *can* measure the length of the long side of a cone from an elevation ◁**12**▷.

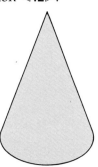

1 Use compasses to draw the circular base of the cone. Divide it into 12 equal segments using a 30°/60° set square.

2 Set the compasses to the side length AB (see <12>). Draw a long arc touching the circle. Then join A to B.

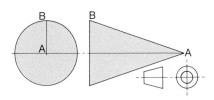

3 Set the compasses to $\frac{1}{12}$ the circumference of the circular base.

Mark off 12 equal lengths along the arc BD. This gives you the point C.

Join A to C to complete the development.

◁**13**▷ *Developing a cone – the base is easily divided into twelve parts using a 30°/60° set square. Then these parts are measured off on the large arc using dividers.*

1 Is ◁**5**▷ the only possible surface development of a cube? If there are others, sketch them.

2 ◁**8**▷ is the development of a square-based pyramid. Sketch the development of a triangle-based pyramid.

3 Sometimes when a circle is used in a construction, twelve reference points are marked around its edge. Why are twelve points marked instead of, say, ten?

4 Construct the development of a cone. Choose its height and diameter yourself.

5 Make a list of everyday objects which have been constructed from developments. Try to include objects made from different materials such as cardboard, metal and plastic.

How to get the shadow right

How shadows are formed

A shadow is formed when an object comes between a light source and other nearby surfaces. The light source may be natural (the sun, a fire), or artificial (a lamp). Surfaces in the shadow have a darker tone because less light is reaching them.

You can use shadows to help show the shape and position of an object. A shadow can show that an object is sitting on a surface, and not floating in space. Shadows can also make your drawings more realistic.

Getting to know shadows

You can either use a simple **construction** to draw a shadow, or you can make an educated guess about its shape, as I have in ◁**1**▷. To do this you need to study shadows whenever you can. Study how they are cast on flat and irregular surfaces.

For a permanent record you could take photographs of the shadows cast by an object when the light source is in different positions. If you have access to a video camera you can trace shadows from a TV screen using the method shown in 3.7 ◁**5**▷.

Shadows from a spotlight

You can **construct** a shadow if you know where the light source is, and where the object casting the shadow is. ◁**2**▷ shows you how to construct the shadow of a pole. ◁**3**▷ shows you how to construct the shadow of a cube by treating each edge as if it were a pole like the one in ◁**2**▷.

Constructing complicated shadows

The lid of the box in ◁**4**▷ is open. This makes the shadow more complicated, but you can still use the method shown in ◁**2**▷ to draw it.

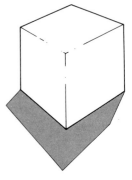

◁**1**▷ *I have drawn this shadow using guesswork and my experience. It's easy to do this for simple objects. The light source, which is higher than the cube, is behind and to the right of it.*

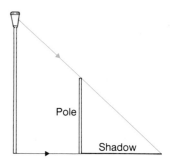

◁**2**▷ *How to construct the shadow of a pole produced by a single light source. If you change the position of the light source the shadow will change.*

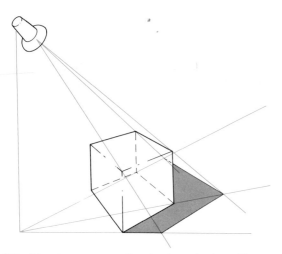

◁**3**▷ *How to construct the shadow of a box. The construction in ◁2▷ is used for each edge of the box. Then the shadow ends are joined together.*

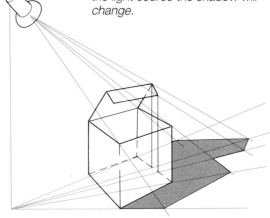

◁**4**▷ *The method shown in ◁3▷ can also be used to draw the shadows of more complicated objects like this open box.*

Shadows from a distant source

When you are outside a building the light source is the sun. It is very far away so you can't show exactly where it is in your drawings. In ◁3▷ and ◁4▷ you can see how the light rays from a nearby source appear to fan out. But the light rays from the sun appear to be parallel. ◁5▷ shows you how the shadow formed by parallel rays is different from the one formed by rays which fan out.

◁6▷ shows the shadows of a cube and an open box formed by parallel light rays. Compare these with ◁3▷ and ◁4▷.

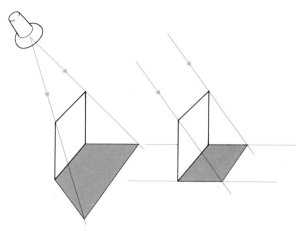

◁**5**▷ *Compare these shadows cast by square sheets of plastic. One is caused by a distant light source, the other by a nearby spotlamp.*

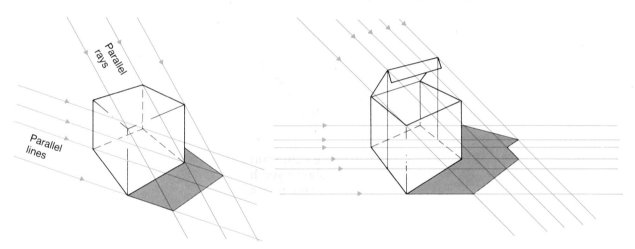

Parallel rays

Parallel lines

◁**6**▷ *Compare these shadows caused by the sun with the spotlight shadows in* ◁3▷ *and* ◁4▷.

Shadows in slots

◁7▷ shows how you can use the same method to draw a shadow in a recess. Imagine that the ground level is brought up to the level of the recess and draw the shadow inside.

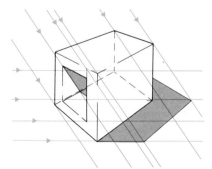

◁**7**▷ *To draw a shadow inside a recess – imagine that ground level has been raised up to the level of the bottom of the recess. Then use the normal construction method.*

1 Sketch a shovel standing in a garden. Add the shadows you would see at these times of day to your sketch:
    • early morning   • midday   • late evening.
2 Light rays drawn from a spotlight appear to 'fan out', but rays from the sun are drawn parallel. Find out why they don't appear to fan out. Write a brief note to explain this to a friend.

3 Make a larger copy of this cylinder. Then try drawing its shadow with a light source in a position of your choice. Tip: treat each line across the end of the cylinder like the pole in ◁2▷. (For more about cylinders see 2.7.)

Exercises on chapter 4

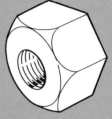

◁**1**▷ *Design a free gift which could be made by encasing a nut like this in acrylic resin.*

1 **Precision Fixings** is a small engineering company which specialises in fastening devices such as nuts, bolts and screws. The company has decided to send various other companies a free gift which will sit on a desk and advertise Precision Fixings' product.

   • The gift should be based on an M30 hexagonal-headed nut encased in a high quality acrylic resin casting.

   • The casting is to be in the shape of a geometrical solid which is different to but complements the hexagon of the nut.

   • The **logo** of the company is to be stamped on each face of the nut.

   You are commissioned to design both the company's logo and the gift. Precision Fixings would like a set of orthographic drawings and a presentation drawing of your designs. They also want to see your initial design ideas in case there is an earlier design which they prefer.

2 Your design for the gift to advertise Precision Fixings has been so successful that you have been asked to design the packaging it will be sent off in. Work out the development of a box which will hold your design securely.

   • The outside of the box is to be of one colour with the company logo and address overprinted in black.

   • Make the finished box from a thin sheet of coloured card.

3 **Precision Fixings** want a symbol to represent their product. They will use it as a **letterhead** at the top of their printed stationery or on a small brochure.

   • They have decided they want a hexagonal-headed screw illuminated with a shaft of light.

   • The company logo is to be incorporated into the shadow cast by the screw.

   When you have worked out the logo design (exercise 1 above) include it in a letterhead with the name Precision Fixings, and an imaginary address.

4 The Russian doll on page 52 has to be manufactured in wood. The production engineer thinks he can make the outer shape of the smallest doll (the solid one) on a lathe with a specially made scraping tool. You are asked to design the shape of the cutting edge on the tool.

   • If the doll is 30 mm high, decide on the exact size and position of all radii required to make the tool.

   • Produce a large scale drawing of the tool showing the centres of the radii and the points of tangency for all the curves.

Using graphics to show data and processes

5

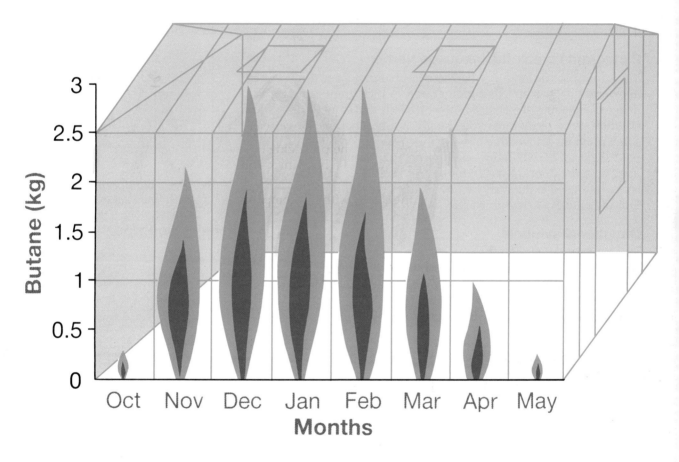

You have been learning how to use graphics to give information about objects. But graphics can also be used to convey messages, to present numeric data or to show processes. Use your imagination—add some flair to your graphics and see if you can get information across at a glance.

Impact graphics

What are impact graphics?

Graphic designs or symbols which get a message across instantly are sometimes called **impact graphics**. The message can be one of warning, assistance or recognition. This style of communication is not a new idea. The Jolly Roger has been used for centuries and is recognised by people of all nationalities. As well as meaning a pirate ship, the skull and crossbones is now used to label poisons and dangerous medicines ◁1▷. They still symbolize danger and death.

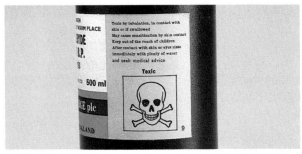

◁**1**▷ The skull and crossbones is a very strong example of **impact graphics**. It symbolizes danger, and is used on poisonous chemicals.

Pictograms break the language barrier

You can break the language barrier and give messages to people of many nationalities by using **pictograms**. A pictogram is a stylised image of a person, object, or event which tells you something quickly.

When using pictograms you usually assume that the viewer has some previous knowledge of what the pictogram represents. Most road signs are based on this assumption. ◁**2**▷ shows the pictograms used on toilet doors. No sign for a toilet itself is shown, but so few rooms are used exclusively by one sex that we all know these signs indicate a toilet or changing area.

◁**2**▷ These **pictograms** of a male and female figure are used on doors to indicate separate male and female facilities e.g. toilets.

Directional symbols

Directional symbols like those in ◁3▷ indicate direction by using different types and shapes of arrows. You can combine words or pictograms with arrows to show where something is. Here are some examples of words used in this way:
Exit, Firepoint, Overhead Conveyor, Volume.

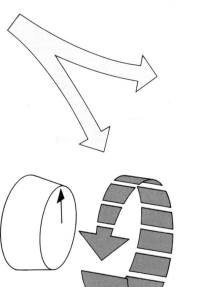

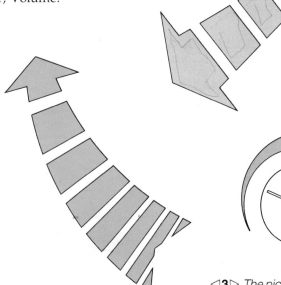

◁**3**▷ The pictorial type of arrow used in a directional symbol is chosen to convey added information.

Logos identify organizations and products

Like pictograms, **logos** are stylized images used to convey messages. Logos tend to be related to a product or organization. You may recognise some of the logos in ◁**4**▷. The Heinemann windmill logo is used on the cover of this book.

◁**5**▷ shows some **logograms** – these are a cross between a logo and a pictogram – the logo itself includes a pictorial representation. In these examples the shapes of the letters have been distorted so that each logo represents the object it describes.

◁**4**▷ *To be effective, logos like these must be instantly recognisable.*

What is a successful logo?

A logo that isn't recognised is almost useless! Most people would recognise logos like the car badges in ◁**4**▷, while most children would recognise the 'transformer' logo in ◁**6**▷. Just about everyone would recognise the LEGO logo in ◁**6**▷. This is an example of a very successful logo. A good logo may also reinforce the image of a product. The Puma logo in ◁**4**▷ is intended to reinforce a sports shoe's image of speed and strength.

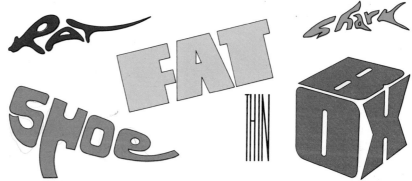

◁**5**▷ *These are just a few examples of logograms which use letters to make pictures. Can you invent some more of your own?*

How do logos work?

A logo only works when you have been taught to link it with a message. The message in an advertisement might be: "Zarbo washing powder shifts stains fast". The name and logo of the powder will appear in the advertisement. The manufacturers hope it will help you remember their product when you are in the supermarket.

Companies and organizations spend a great deal of time and money making sure that their logos are recognised.

◁**6**▷ *Logos used in the toy industry are recognised easily by children.*

---

1 Some logograms are used for warnings, others for instructions. Draw an example of each type.

2 Design a logo for a holiday camp. Design another for a technological institution.

3 The particular shape of a roadsign (circle, triangle, etc.) has a meaning. What is the meaning of each different shape? Why do you think different shapes are used? Design a road sign which warns of possible forest fires and another which forbids you to pass because of an actual forest fire.

Ways of showing data

Rush hour madness

Every day, several hundred people are killed or seriously injured in road accidents in Britain ◁1▷. At some times of day there are many more accidents than others. But you have to look at this table quite closely to see when they are.

◁1▷ *This table shows the average number of people killed or seriously injured in road accidents at different times of the day.*

Time of day	Midnight											Noon
	12–1	1–2	2–3	3–4	4–5	5–6	6–7	7–8	8–9	9–10	10–11	11–12
Seriously injured or killed	6	4	3	1	2	1	3	12	16	10	10	11
Time of day	Noon											Midnight
	12–1	1–2	2–3	3–4	4–5	5–6	6–7	7–8	8–9	9–10	10–11	11–12
Seriously injured or killed	14	14	13	23	26	25	18	16	14	14	15	18

Bar charts help you spot patterns

If you wanted to show the information in ◁1▷ more clearly, you could use a **bar chart**. A bar chart shows how one thing **varies** with another. For example, the bar chart in ◁2▷ shows how the number of accidents every hour varies, depending on the time of day.

The horizontal axis is called the **x axis** and the vertical axis the **y axis**. On the chart in ◁2▷, the y axis shows the number of people injured and the x axis shows the time in hours. So the length of each bar represents the number of people injured in each hour.

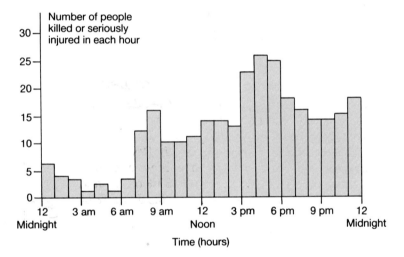

◁2▷ *This chart gives the same information as the table in ◁1▷ but it shows you at a glance when there are most accidents.*

Ordered and disordered data

Look at the bar chart in ◁2▷. Moving from left to right along the x axis, the bars show the numbers of people injured at later and later times. There is an order to the figures on the x axis, and the time interval between the figures is a fixed length of time. The x axis is normally used for ordered figures that increase in steps by a set amount, working from left to right.

Now look at ◁3▷. In this bar chart the y axis shows book prices and the x axis shows book titles. The titles aren't in any particular order, though they could have been ordered alphabetically.

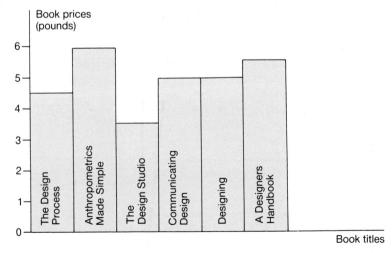

◁3▷ *The x axis on this bar chart shows book titles – they are not in any particular order. Compare it with the x axis in ◁2▷.*

When to use an xy graph

Another way of showing numerical information is to draw a simple **xy** graph. You may have used these in mathematics. You normally use a graph only when the x axis is used for ordered figures that increase in steps by set amounts. You could use an xy graph to show the data on the bar chart in ◁**2**▷. Can you see why it wouldn't be such a good idea to use an xy graph to show the information in ◁**3**▷?

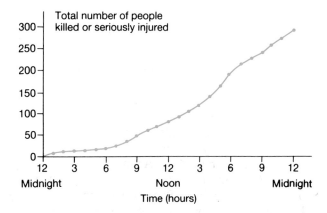

◁**4**▷ *This xy graph shows how the number of people killed or seriously injured increases throughout the day.*

What is data?

Tables, bar charts and graphs are all ways of showing **data**. Data are facts which give information about something. For example, here is some data about Linda: she is 15 yrs old, 1.77 m tall, has black hair and lives in Wigan.

Data is often concerned with quantities: how many? how old? how tall? – so numbers are used. This is known as **numeric** data. But not all data is numeric data. Sometimes data is given in words: what colour? where?

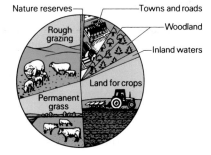

◁**5**▷ *This pie chart shows how land is used in Britain. The size of each segment shows what percentage of the land is used for a particular purpose.*

Pie charts show how things are shared

There are many ways of showing data other than on graphs and bar charts. The pie chart in ◁**5**▷ shows data about land use in Britain. The complete circle represents all the land in Britain (100%). The circle has been divided up to show how much of the land is used for what purpose. 30% of the land in Britain is rough grazing land, so this fills 30% of the circle.

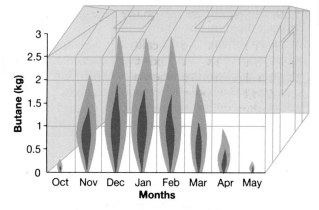

Adding impact to your charts

Look again at the pie chart in ◁**5**▷. The artist has added pictures to the chart to draw attention to it and to show what the chart is about.

You can add impact to a bar chart by replacing the bars with a drawing which represents the data. For example, in the bar chart in ◁**6**▷ the bars have been replaced by flames of different heights.

◁**6**▷ *This pictorial bar chart shows the fuel requirements in a greenhouse. The heights of the flames show how much fuel is used each month.*

---

1 Between what times of day are there most road accidents? Why do you think this is? At what other times of day are there a lot of accidents?

2 Would you use a bar chart, a graph or a pie chart to show
  • the cost per tonne of different materials?
  • the daily sales of a book over a month?
  • how electricity is used in Britain?
  • how the speed of a car changes as it moves away from traffic lights?

3 Draw a pie chart to show how you spend a typical school day. Think of a day as 24 hours. How many hours do you spend studying, watching television, playing sport, asleep? Add pictures to your chart to give it more impact.

More ways of showing data

Polar graphs

A polar graph is a way of representing data on two varying quantities. Polar graphs are often used to show something varying with hours in a day or compass direction so the scale going round the circle is a clock face or compass points. They are often used at viewing points in the countryside to show landmarks. In these sorts of graphs (see ◁**1**▷) a line points in the direction of each landmark towards the compass. The length of the line indicates how distant the landmark is from the viewing point.

In the example in ◁**2**▷ the polar graph has been used to show maximum and minimum temperatures for the twelve months of the year. The months are ranged around the circumference. The outer line shows the maximum temperatures, and the inner line shows the minimum temperatures. Does this polar graph show data from the Northern or Southern hemisphere of the world?

Block diagrams

A block diagram also shows how two things vary with each other. The diagram in ◁**3**▷ shows how much land value varies in a particular area. The value of the land is plotted in 3D on a map of the location of the land. So the diagram gives information on the shape and area of land of different values.

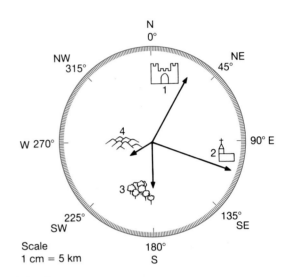

◁**1**▷ A polar graph showing the position and distance of various landmarks from a viewing point.

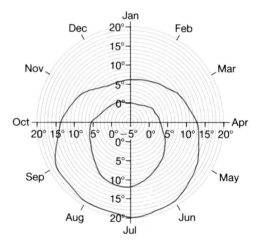

◁**2**▷ A polar graph showing changes in maximum and minimum temperature for each month.

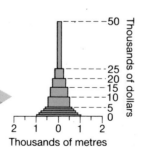

◁**3**▷ This block diagram shows how much land is worth in different parts of an urban area of Kansas, USA.

Pictorial charts to make predictions

You can use charts and graphs to show predictions about data i.e. to show what you think *will* happen, say to the height of a tree or the amount of traffic on a road, in the future. ◁4▷ shows how high I think the trees and shrubs in my garden will grow over the next 30 years. The predicted heights after 5–30 years are shown by the different colours. The colours are explained in the key. The final outlines show when I expect the trees to reach full growth. Some of the trees or shrubs might stop growing well before the others reach maturity. This is shown by the colour shading in each case.

◁4▷ *You can use this sort of predictive graph to help plan a garden . . . assuming you intend to be around to see it!*

Key
- 5 years
- 10 years
- 20 years
- 30 years

Horse Chestnut

Norway Spruce

More information on maps

You can also use graphics to add numeric data to a simple map or diagram. Suppose you want to show the direction of a route on a map and also how often the route is used. You can do this using a **flow diagram**. (Be careful that you do not mix up flow diagrams and flow charts which are different see p.70.) In a flow diagram you vary the width of a road or route to show how much it is used. So a well used path is drawn very thick compared to a little used path which is drawn very thin. You can give a scale to make the information more precise.

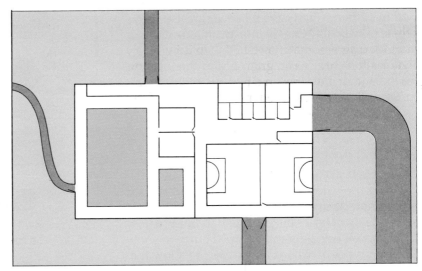

◁5▷ *This flow diagram shows the amount that different routes to and from a sports centre are used. This can be helpful in redesigning buildings and surrounding walkways.*

1 If grass needs 4°C to grow, when do you think I will need to start cutting the lawn? Use the polar diagram in ◁2▷ .
2 Draw a flow diagram to show the number of people walking around *part* of your school at a particular time of day. For example show the different directions taken by pupils when they arrive, depart and move between a certain lesson.
3 Use a block diagram to show the prices of seats at your local concert hall or football ground.

How to show processes

Showing how an organization works

Government departments, schools and companies are often large organizations with hundreds of people in them. Have you ever wondered how much the people at the top of an organization – the managing directors and headteachers – know about the people they work with? And how does important information get from the bottom to the top (or from top to bottom) of an organization?

In most organizations, people work in groups for a **manager** of some kind. The manager of a production line will communicate information about company policy to the people she works with. And they may communicate their ideas for improving the product to the manager, who will pass on the ideas to other people in the organization.

The structure of an organization can be shown in an **organization** chart. ◁1▷ is a school organization chart. It shows how a headteacher could have found out that a student has won the local marathon. Charts like this one can also show people exactly how they fit into an organization. A chart like this is sometimes called a military organization chart because the nearer the top you are the higher your 'rank' is! Not all organizations are structured in the same way.

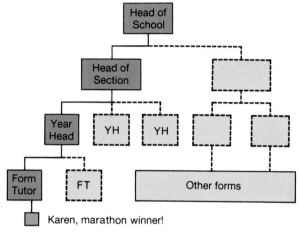

◁**1**▷ This organization chart shows how information is passed to the headteacher. See how the message about the marathon win is passed up through the ranks.

Showing processes with flow charts

Flow charts like ◁2▷ are a convenient way of showing the order in which a task or set of tasks is carried out. As in organization charts the diagrams are made up of boxes linked together. But in a flow diagram you use differently shaped boxes to show different types of actions and arrows to show the direction in which to work through the chart.

◁2▷ shows a simple flow chart of how any task could be represented. You first have to *start*. Then you do the first *process*. You ask yourself a *question*: Have I done it right? If the answer is *yes*, you go to the next process, if *no* then try it again. This continues until you have achieved what you wanted to do. Notice how you can add notes in brackets at the side of a box to explain more about what happens in each box.

The flow chart must be able to lead you right through *any possible sequence* for completing the task.

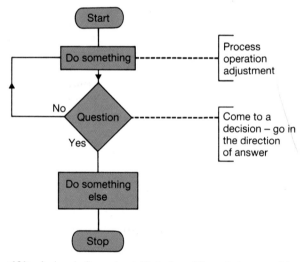

◁**2**▷ A simple flow chart. Note the different shapes of the start, process and decision boxes.

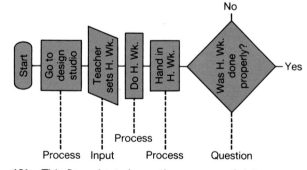

◁**3**▷ This flow chart shows the process of doing your D + T homework! The chart is not very detailed. What other information would you add to it?

Showing processes in picture form

You can also use a series of pictograms like the ones described in Section 5.1 to show how to operate a machine or perform a task. These are very useful for people who do not read or speak the language. The sequence in ◁4▷ shows how to make a call from an old-style public telephone box. The process is now a bit different in new phone boxes. Could you draw a series of pictures to show the present day process?

◁4▷ This sequence of drawings shows how to operate on old-style public telephone. Do you understand the instructions in each frame?

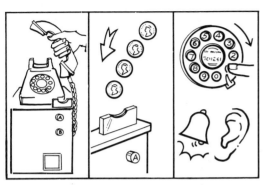

Either....

or....

Designing using process drawings

A process drawing is a type of plan which shows both lay-out and movement. The **process drawing** of the kitchen in ◁5▷ shows that it is badly designed. The three items used most often in a kitchen are the sink, the cooker and the refrigerator. You can see from the **triangle of movement** in the drawing that these three things are just about as far apart as they can be, making life in the kitchen very tiresome!

To redesign a better kitchen you should first make a list of all the things that people do there and the main items needed. Then draw a plan showing the various items and include lines linking all the necessary movements together. In this way you can judge whether you have come up with a sensible and convenient arrangement . . . or play around with your plan to improve it. Remember not to put water and electricity too close together!

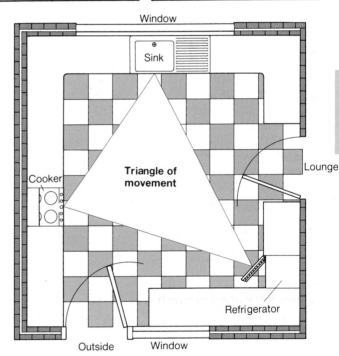

◁5▷ You would have to walk quite a long way if you were preparing a meal in this kitchen!

1 The basic boxes in a flow chart are stop, start, process, input and question. Use these to draw a flow chart showing how to half fill a sink with luke-warm water from the hot and cold taps.

2 In industry, the person responsible for organizing working processes is called a **works study** specialist. Look at how materials are stored and distributed in your design studio. Make a process diagram showing how you would improve the system.

3 Sequential drawings are used a lot at international airports. Make a sequence drawing for display at a bus terminus at a British airport explaining how a driver-only bus service might operate.

Exercises on chapter 5

1 Your toy firm has just introduced a new range of fantasy toys based on futuristic android sea creatures. You need to design identification badges for both the good and the bad creatures. It should be clear from the style of the badge which is for the good and which for the bad creatures.

2 Conduct a survey of the types of cars in the school car park. You could divide them into saloons, hatchbacks, estates and sports cars. Make a chart to show the results, using visual images to represent the different types. Could you add extra information to your chart? Perhaps you could include engine size or the letter showing the registration year?

3 Pick an area of grass in the school grounds. Show the distribution of clover in this area as a block diagram. Decide on a scale before you start.

4 Make a simple plan of the layout of your design studio or drawing office on graph paper. Now make a chart to show your teacher's movements during a typical lesson. Redesign the studio layout to make it (a) easier for the teacher to get to the students (b) easier for the students to get to the kit, computer and photocopier.

5 Produce a set of sequential drawings showing how to start up your departmental computer.

6 You have set up the pillar drill in the school workshop ready for drilling. You press the contactor and nothing happens. Draw a flow chart to show the sequence you would go through to see why the drill does not operate.

Modelling and model making

Another way of presenting your designs or of testing out your ideas is by modelling. As with drawing, there are many different modelling techniques. This chapter looks at some of these techniques and the tools you will need.

Tools for modelling

What materials do you need to model?

You will see from the range of materials in this section that you can model with almost anything. However, it is always easier if you have the right tools and materials for the job. Certain tools are for use with certain materials. Most of the tools illustrated on this page can be found in a school workshop but some are specialist tools, designed to help you work more quickly and efficiently.

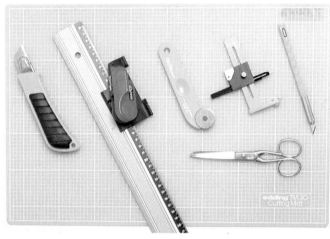

◁**1**▷ *You use these tools mainly for cutting paper and card. You must keep them sharp for model work – and take care!*

What is the equipment used for?

Modelling, like sketching and illustrating, is another way for you to work out your design ideas and communicate them to others. There are different modelling techniques just as there are different drawing techniques. Once you have decided *why* you want to make a model, then you can judge what type of model will be best to make.

As you can see, the equipment on this page is very varied – you can make a simple model from paper and card or model in idea form on a computer. Some of the equipment shown here is for use only in the final stages of modelling.

As a designer you need to understand how and when to use different techniques and choose the materials and equipment to suit your aims.

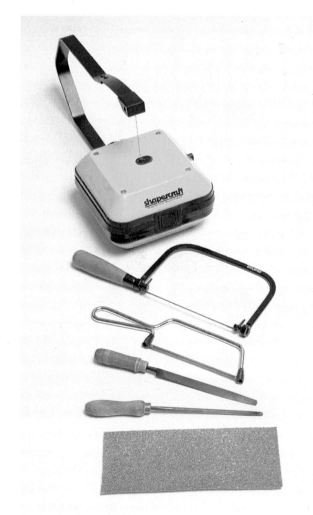

◁**2**▷ *You use these tools for shaping and cutting hard materials like wood, metal and plastic. Small work tools are often useful for modelling.*

Taking care of equipment

It is very important to take care of the tools and equipment you are using. It is hard to work accurately with equipment which is not well maintained. For example you will not produce good models unless your edge tools are extremely sharp and your work area is kept tidy. Also some of the equipment you use is quite expensive – another reason why you should look after it carefully. If you are careful, tidy and accurate you will be able to achieve your best result.

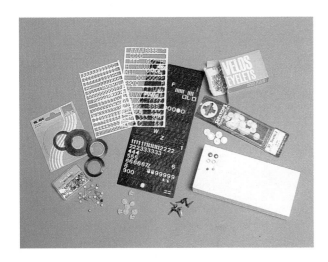

◁3▷ *You can add interesting texture and detail to a model before you paint it using materials like these. Always be on the look-out for other materials that you can use in this way.*

◁4▷ *When your model is finished you can paint it using equipment like this. Your model should be of high quality before it is painted.*

◁5▷ *You can use a computer to make a model on screen. The computer must be a powerful one for most computer modelling. Some suitable systems are now available in schools. Has your school got one?*

1 Can you name all the apparatus on this page? If not, ask your teacher to help you.
2 There are many other tools and materials which you can use for modelling. Make a list of others not shown here and what you use them for. Think about tools you may have used to make models at home. Share the information with the rest of your group.

Block modelling

What is block modelling?

Block models are solid three dimensional models which give a good idea of the *size*, *shape*, *form* and *look* of your design. They are usually made out of lightweight, durable, solid materials like expanded polystyrene (see ◁**5**▷). You can see from ◁**1**▷ that a block model does not need to have a great deal of detail. But the model of the personal stereo does allow you to see the arrangement of the controls, which are on several surfaces and gives you a good 'feel' for the overall design. The same information could be shown on a set of drawings but it would not be so clear and immediate.

◁**1**▷ *A block model of a personal stereo made from styrofoam. The details were added using card and paint.*

Block modelling to reduced scale

Block modelling is also useful for making scale models to illustrate **spatial relationships**, say in a bathroom or kitchen. High density styrofoam was used to make the model of the bathroom in ◁**2**▷. The model shows how the various items in the bathroom fit together. Quite a bit of detail has been included in this model to give a good impression of what the bathroom will actually be like. The designer could have made a single point perspective drawing (see p.22) to show the same arrangement. But the model allows you to view the room from different angles and get a feeling of the space and lay-out.

The model of the car in ◁**3**▷ has also been made to scale. In this case a block model was made because the complexity of the curves on the car's body would be difficult to show in a drawing.

◁**2**▷ *A scale model of a bathroom. Each item is modelled in high density styrofoam and is arranged to show how the room would look in real life.*

Block modelling to test fit and size

Block modelling is very useful when you want to test how easy something is for a person to use, say a tool or toy. In ◁**4**▷ the block model of a power drill has been made to help work out the best shape for the handle. Only the hand-grip of the drill was being considered, so only that part was modelled in finished form.

◁**3**▷ *A model car made from expanded polystyrene. It has been coated with a mixture of PVA and Polyfilla before being spray painted to give an elegant finish.*

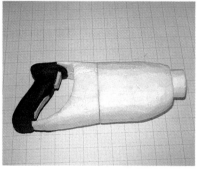

◁**4**▷ *The main body of this power drill has been roughly modelled in expanded polystyrene. The handle has been shaped and finished properly. Gouache has been used to give a coloured matt effect.*

Which materials are best for block models?

For block modelling you need materials that have depth, are light and are easy to shape. They must be safe to work with and easy to bring to a good finish. When choosing a material for use on a school project or at home you will also need to consider the price of the material. ◁**5**▷ shows some suitable materials which should fit your price range. Try to be on the lookout for other materials which you could use.

◁**5**▷ *High density styrofoam, expanded polystyrene and polyurethane foam are all suitable materials for block modelling. You can also use the timbers, jelutong and balsa.*

Rules for block modelling

When doing block modelling you should follow the same guidelines as usual when working.

- Keep everything clean and tidy.
- Pay careful attention to safety. Check whether you should take precautions with materials and tools you are using. (See table). It is a good rule always to wear a mask when working with plastic dusts and to wear goggles when using machines. Some materials give off less dust if you work with them when damp. This can also improve the quality of the finish.
- Before experimenting with new materials ask your teacher for advice.
- Always experiment with glues and paints on scraps of the material before you use them on your model.
- Be economic. Remember why you are making the model. You are simply trying to get a feel for the shape, style and size of the design, not make a perfect prototype. You may be able to achieve this without too much time consuming and expensive 'finishing off'.

◁**6**▷ *A polyurethane foam model used to investigate shapes for a caravan.*

	① Cutting				② Bonding					③ Smoothing					④ Filling				⑤ Sealing		⑥ Finishing							⑦ Health & Safety	
	Bandsaw	Shapercraft saw	Coping saw	Modelling knife	PVA	Epoxy	Impact	Hot melt	D/S sellotape	Rasp	File	Glass paper	Wet & dry—wet	Wet & dry—dry	Cellulose filler	Cellulose filler + PVA	Car bodyfiller	Plasticine	PVA	Emulsion	Plaka	Plaka-lac	Gouache	Emulsion	Enamel spray	Enamel paint	Cellulose spray	Dust problem	Fume problem
High density styrofoam	•	•	•	•	•		•		•	•	•	•	•	•	•	•		•	•	•	•	•	•	•	○	•	○	•	•
Expanded polystyrene	•	•	•	•	•		•		•		•	•			•	•		•	•	•	•	•	•	•	○	•	○	•	•
Polyurethane Foam	•	•	•		•	•				•	•	•	•	•					•	•				•	•	•	•	•	
Jelutong	•	•	•	•						•	•	•	•	•					•					•	•	•	•	•	
Balsa	•	•	•	•	•				•	•	•	•	•	•					•					•	•	•	•		

Checklist of materials

The table above lists various materials which are suitable for block modelling and shows how they should be worked, at each stage of the modelling process. Health and safety factors are also highlighted (column 7).

1. Each of the five models in ◁**1**▷ to ◁**4**▷ and ◁**6**▷ have been made for a purpose. Give the purpose in each case and say how you think it has been achieved.
2. Why should you know how glues and paints work on various modelling materials? Say what you would use to bond and finish a model made from polyurethane foam.
3. Study the table. Which material would you think was the most useful and easy to use for block modelling? Give your reasons. Why do you think different materials are used?

Modelling with sheet materials

Why model with sheet materials?

The **sheet materials** used for modelling start off as flat pieces of card, wood, plastic or metal. They might be bent into simple curved shapes, or moulded into more complicated shapes in the modelling process. The most commonly used sheet materials have a high quality surface finish, which may be smooth or textured.

Some sheet materials, especially those that bend when heated, can be **vacuum formed** to produce curves. Though the top and bottom surfaces of these materials are finished to a high quality already, the edges are often unfinished and difficult for you to finish off.

Sheet materials are useful for making models which need to show the construction of the inside and outside of a design, see ◁1▷, ◁2▷ and ◁4▷. The material is built up to make a 'shell' (a hollow structure). This is called **fabrication**. The construction method can save you time compared to what it would take to make a block model with a quality finish, and can show much more of the detail.

The material you use should be the one most suited to the model you are realizing.

Imitating a final construction

◁1▷ shows a model in sheet card which was made to work out the construction of a bathroom 'tidy'. The design, the cutting and folding of the material etc, is worked out on the model using cardboard – a cheaper but similar material to the one to be used for the design – to see if the idea works. If you use exactly the same material for the model as for the actual product your model will be a **prototype**.

Hollow box models

The hollow box model of a flash gun in ◁2▷ is made from **kapa board** – a thin foamed sheet, faced with cardboard on both sides. This is known as a **composite** material. Kapa board is a useful material for modelling because it can easily be shaped by **kerfing** ◁3▷, and bonded using an electric glue gun. The model in ◁2▷ could have been made more durable and to a higher standard by using polystyrene sheet. However, kapa board is faster and cheaper to use. You can spray models made from both these sheet materials – kapa board and polystyrene sheet – with cellulose car paint whereas styrene foam block models would dissolve in the solvent.

Architectural models

The complicated architectural model in ◁4▷ has been fabricated from card. Quite a lot of detail has been included to give a very lively and 'real' finished effect. Models of buildings are often made so that sections and roofs can be removed to show the intended lay-out *inside* the building.

◁1▷ *Cardboard model of a bathroom sink tidy.*

◁2▷ *Kapa board model of a flash gun.*

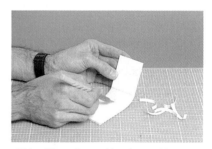

◁3▷ *Kapa board is shaped by a process known as **kerfing**. The bottom layer of card is removed. The material is bent smoothly.*

◁4▷ *Architect's model of Broxborne Civic Centre.*

Which sheet materials are best for modelling?

A wide range of sheet materials is available for modelling. You should choose an inexpensive material which is suitable for your model, which you can work with and which will give you a good quality finish. You can use materials ranging through wood, metal, plastic and composite boards. Tables ◁5▷ and ◁6▷ give details of sheet modelling materials you can use.

◁**5**▷ *Table showing the composition of various sheet materials.*

Material	Nature	Direction	Modelling thickness
Hardboard	Compressed timber fibres	No	3–6 mm
Plywood	Bonded timber laminates with alternating grain	No	1.5–6 mm**
Veneer	Thin timber sheet	Yes	1–2 mm
Millboard	Rough finish cardboard	No	1–2 mm
Folding box board	Smooth hard finish with soft centre	No	200–400 gsm
Manilla card	Smooth hard finish	No	100 gsm
Kapa board	Polypropylene foam laminate between box board	No	2–6 mm
Foam board	Polystyrene foam laminate between box board	No	2–6 mm
High impact styrene	Solid sheet plastic, hard, dense and brittle	No	1–5 mm
ABS	Solid sheet plastic, hard, dense and fairly brittle	No	1–5 mm
Acrylic	Solid sheet plastic, hard, dense and fairly brittle	No	1–5 mm**
Fluted polypropylene	Corrugated plastic sheet, stiff, hollow	Yes	3–5 mm
PVC Foam	Polyvinyl chloride foam, various densities	No	1–5 mm**

**other sizes available

◁**6**▷ *Table showing the various stages of working with each sheet material.*

	Cutting						Bending			Bonding											Smoothing					Edging			Finishing							
	Shaper saw	Coping saw	Modelling knife	Scratch & snap	Perforation cutter	Mitre cutter	Hot	Cold	Kerf	PVA	Epoxy-Rapide	PVC	Impact	Rubber	Hot melt	Tensol	Liquid poly	EMA plastic weld	Spraymount	Pritt/Peli-fix	File	Glass paper	Wet & dry	Buffing	Not reqd	Bonded strip	Bodyfiller	Polyfiller	Enamel	Cellulose	PVA	Emulsion	Water	Water	Spirit
Hardboard	●	●								●	●	●	●	●							●	●	●			●			●	●	●	●			
Plywood	●	●						●	●	●	●	●	●	●							●	●					●		●	●	●	●	●		
Veneer	●		●			●		●		●	●	●	●	●					●		●	●							●	●	●	●			
Mill board	●		●			●	●	●	●	●	●	●	●						●		●	●	●						●	●	●	●	●	●	●
Folding box board	●		●	●	●		●		●	●	●	●	●						●	●						●		●	●	●	●	●	●	●	●
Manilla card			●	●	●	●		●		●		●	●						●	●						●			●	●	●	●	●	●	●
Kapa board	●		●			●		●		●	●	●	●						●		●	●	●			●	●		●	●	●		●	●	
Foam board	●		●			●		●	●	●											●	●				●	●	●	●	●	●		●	●	
High impact styrene		●	●	●			●								●	●			●	●		●	●	●					●						●
ABS		●	●	●			●									●			●			●	●	●					●						●
Acrylic		●	●	●			●										●					●	●	●					●						●
Fluted polypropylene	●		●				●							●				●				●				●	●		●						●
PVC foam	●	●	●	●			●				●	●	●					●			●	●		●					●	●					●

---

1 What do you think the heading 'Direction' in table ◁5▷ means? What does this apply to in the case of a) veneer, b) fluted polypropylene?

2 Why do you have to pay attention to the edge of some of these sheet materials? Suggest ways of overcoming the problem in different materials.

3 In Section 6.2 ◁1▷, a sheet material (cardboard) was used with a block material. Give an example of a model you could make in which you could use the quality of surface finish on a sheet to 'improve' a block model.

Modelling to work out ideas

Sketch modelling

You are probably already used to sketching ideas on paper. You may use these to build up to a final drawing or model. But sometimes you need to test your ideas further to see if they will work. You can do this by making models which will let you see how things go together. This is called **sketch modelling**. Sketching is quick, but accurate drawing. Sketch modelling is quick, but accurate modelling!

What do you need for sketch modelling?

Sketch models are for your own use. They are to help you work out ideas and are not meant to be finished off like presentation models. However, they should be good enough to allow others to follow your ideas through. ◁1▷ shows equipment that you might use for sketch modelling. All these bits and pieces are suitable for quick and easy working. An electric glue gun will give you instant bonding and eyelets and a punch allow you to make moving joints quickly. If you use these items together with some of the cheap sheet materials listed in table ◁5▷ on p.79, you can make very useful sketch models.

◁1▷ *Useful equipment for sketch modelling.*

Sketch modelling to work out linkages

In any model of a moving object (or person!) you will need to join the moving parts by a **link mechanism**. ◁2▷ shows a sketch model of a face which is designed to move. The idea could have been worked out on paper but the sketch model allows you to find the right size and position for each part. The model also lets you see if the mechanism works, so you can evaluate and, if necessary, alter your idea as you go along. But remember – the model must be accurate to be useful.

◁2▷ *A sketch model to work out linkages. Get the size of the linkage right first, then work out the shapes.*

Part modelling

You make a sketch model to help you work out an idea or to understand something. So you only have to model enough to make this possible. The model in ◁3▷ represents *part* of a sewing machine. It was made to investigate the cloth feed mechanism on a machine. This is a part model. To understand the working of this one mechanism you don't have to model the whole machine.

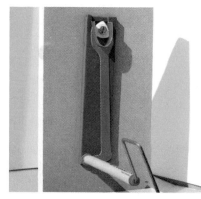

◁3▷ *A model to investigate the cloth feed on a sewing machine.*

Sketch modelling of a mechanism

The two pictures in ◁4▷ show a model of a toy rowing boat. This is a complete sketch model. The model is of the whole mechanism. You could measure from this model and work out details of the shape and form of individual parts which would make the final design look more realistic.

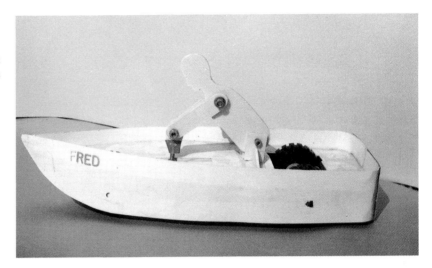

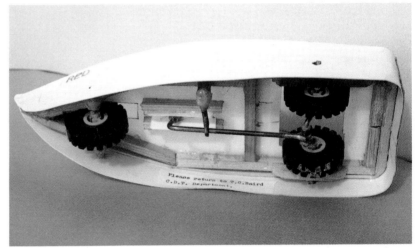

◁4▷ A sketch model to work out the mechanisms for a toy rowboat. The two pictures show the model from different viewpoints.

Sketch modelling for form

Quick sketch modelling is also very useful for working out shape or form, especially where complicated curves are involved. If you use a very plastic material like clay or plasticine, you can rough out the essential features of a design before you refine them. ◁5▷ shows some rough polyurethane foam models of a caravan before it was refined by the designer. You can see that the finished model ◁6▷ shows a great deal of detail but the location of the important curves shown on the sketch model has been retained. It would be very difficult to show this complex form in a drawing.

◁5▷ Sketch models showing the rough shape and form for a caravan.

◁6▷ A block model of the caravan worked to a finish, showing final details.

1 Why might you make a sketch model when you are designing a toy with moving parts? Model a man on a push bike using cardboard to see how this model could help you towards a final design.
2 Look at tables ◁5▷ and ◁6▷ in Section 6.3 and list the materials given which you could also use for making sketch models.
3 When would clay be helpful in sketch modelling? Model a joy stick for a computer game using clay or plasticine.

Modelling with construction kits

Using construction kits

You can buy different commercial construction kits, like LEGO or Fischer Technik in model shops and toy shops. You can use these kits to make a model by following an idea and a set of instructions provided by the manufacturer (see Section 2.10 ◁1▷). However you can also use these kits to make models to work out and test *your own* ideas.

It is helpful to make the manufacturer's set models so that you gain confidence with the kit and discover its scope. You can then use it with ease when modelling your own designs. You can also use kits to test ideas because you can dismantle and reassemble construction kit models relatively quickly.

Using a kit for modelling

You may decide to use a kit to model a design and to see if it will work. But remember the makers of these kits are trying to suit a lot of people, some of whom simply want to have fun with them. So you may not find everything you need in a kit. At times you may have to add to or modify a part to complete your model. Ask your teacher before you do this. However, by combining the use of a kit with other modelling skills and materials, you will gain flexibility for your work.

Designing mechanical ideas with kits

You will probably use kits mainly for designing things that move. When you use a kit to try out an idea, your model may not look elegant but this doesn't matter. You can add style later.

Some pupils were asked to design a toy swimming creature which had rotating arms and alternately moving legs. So the design needed a mechanism to make the arms go round and the legs go up and down. ◁2▷ shows their solution for the mechanism made from a LEGO kit. This is a working solution. ◁3▷ shows the block model they made to design the exterior. By modifying the mechanism so that it fits into this block body shell (or *vice versa*), the pupils could make a working prototype of the final design.

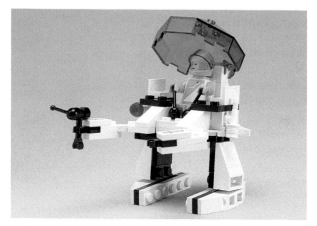

◁**1**▷ *This is a LEGO model built using instructions provided by the manufacturers. You will get some idea of what the kit can do when you build models like these.*

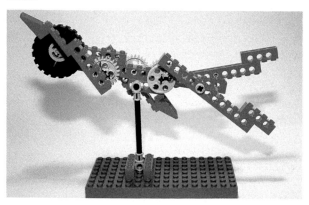

◁**2**▷ *This mechanism for a swimming toy with rotating arms and moving legs was built from LEGO. The design was worked out without using manufacturer's instructions.*

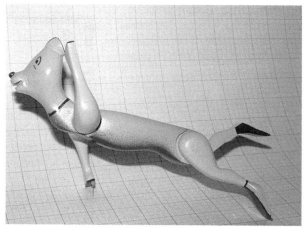

◁**3**▷ *Body shell block model for the swimming toy in ◁2▷. This model is made from styrofoam.*

Using kits to understand mechanical principles

Most kits come with instructions on how to construct some standard mechanisms for making things move, using their system (see ◁4▷). These are useful in helping you understand how certain mechanical principles work and how the parts go together. You can experiment with these different standard mechanical systems. When you understand them you can modify them to suit your own designs.

◁4▷ *Kit manufacturers usually give you instructions on how to assemble a range of standard mechanisms. It is fun to try them out.*

Kits as test rigs

You can use kits to make a **test rig** to try out a particular mechanical principle. Fischer Technik was used to make the test rig for **cams** (circular discs which convert rotational motion to up and down motion (shown in ◁5▷)). The cams are made from millboard and are fastened to the Fischer Technik rig. When the cam under test is rotated you can see exactly how it works. So this simple rig allows you to test various cam sizes by trial and error. Once you have finalised the basic shape of the cam in this way you can then include an accurate construction drawing of it in your complete design.

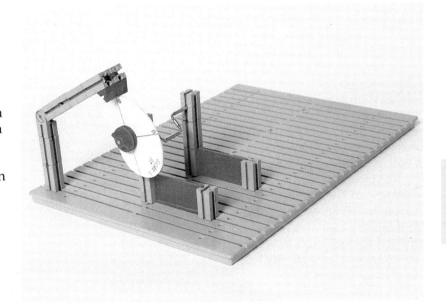

◁5▷ *A simple Fischer Technik assembly makes a good test rig for cams.*

To answer these questions you will need to use construction kits.

1 The sketch model shown in ◁4▷ in Section 6.4 uses LEGO wheels and mild steel rods for the mechanism. Try to work out how to do the job using just LEGO parts. *Remember*: to explain the mechanism it is not necessary to show the shape of the boat.

2 Some kits are good for making models which have parts under tension (a force stretching them apart) and some for parts that are in compression (a force squeezing them together). Using suitable parts from a kit set up different models to show examples of tension and compression.

3 Design a simple gear box in which the *driven* gear wheel is rotating at three times the speed of the *driver* gear wheel. Make the gear box using two or three different kits to see which is the easiest to use.

Presentation models

What is a presentation model?

A presentation model is a very accurate model of your design which gives a realistic, visual impression of the actual finished product. Such a model should include all the details of the trial product. A presentation model is often meant to be handled and assessed by others (see ◁1▷). It's as if you are saying. 'This is exactly how my design is going to be, pick it up and look at it.'

When should you make a presentation model?

A presentation model is made near the end of the design process. By then you will have decided on the size, shape, mechanism, final materials and colour for your product. The presentation model should show if your design works visually – if it looks as good as you intended – and if it will appeal to others. It may, however, show you that your design is not quite right and that you must change a certain detail or details of your work.

Any old models?

People have been making presentation models to show designs for hundreds of years. These were often scale models, used instead of formal orthographic drawings to give an accurate impression of the intended product. A designer would either do a detailed painting or a presentation model – for everything from furniture to battleships – to show the buyer what they were getting! The models had to be accurate and visually pleasing so the designer could convince the rich to place their orders!

◁1▷ This presentation model gives a realistic impression of a flash-gun.

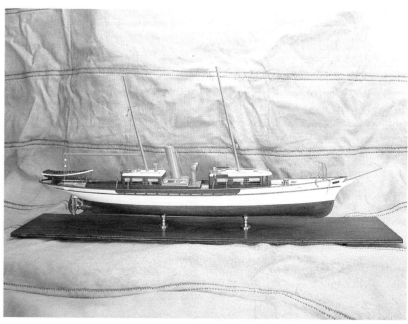

◁2▷ This model gives you all the details of the ship without the need to read or understand orthographic drawings.

Prototype models

Sooner or later you will want to make the actual product that you have spent so long designing! If it is a one-off item, you will simply manufacture it and end up with a **working prototype**. If you were making one special table this would be the end of the process but if you wanted to make 1000 tables, all exactly the same, you would make the prototype and then set up a production line to produce all the tables. As a general rule, a prototype does *everything* required of the product and is the final size while a presentation model is visually accurate but doesn't work or is not to scale. However you should try to produce your presentation models to full size wherever possible.

Materials for presentation models

You will find that many of the techniques and materials used in block and sheet modelling can be used for presentation models. But you must always choose a material that can be finished to a very high quality.

Adding detail

If you look carefully at any pocket calculator you will see that the design is very detailed. The external faces of a calculator are not just plain sheets of plastic but contain raised or lowered surfaces, textures and patterns. There may be screws, holes to take screws, raised feet and a battery compartment at the back. There may be lines where different bits of plastic join. When making a presentation model of such a product you need to show all these details using anything that is available! Use your imagination and have fun – self adhesive labels, line tapes, textured paper, plastic plugs, buttons, can all be stuck on and sprayed with paint. They will give a realistic representation of the textures and detail of your product. ◁**3**▷ in section 6.1 will give you some idea of what you can use.

◁**3**▷ *This table has been made by machine. A prototype would have been made before it went into mass production.*

◁**4**▷ *This pocket calculator has an injection moulded plastic case. Notice all the details the design includes.*

1 Look carefully at a pocket calculator. Make sketches of it and label all the features that you would include in a presentation model.
2 Pocket calculators have buttons. Make a list of readily available items that you could paint and use to represent the buttons on a presentation model of a calculator.
3 Although it is preferable to make a full size presentation model, sometimes a scale model is best. List some examples of when this would be the case.

Modelling using computers

Models made simple

Some of your final designs may be quite complicated. At times you may get too bogged down in all this detail to think through a certain part of the design. However, you can solve a particular design problem by making a simplified model which clears away a lot of the clutter! Once you have worked out your ideas on the simplified model you can then apply this to your original design. This is similar to how you use sketch models to work out mechanisms (see Section 6.4). In these sketch models you remove the added complication of the final form and reduce the model to just the basic parts and simple mechanisms.

Modelling on a micro-computer

You can use a microcomputer to make simplified models which can then be built up and investigated on the computer. ◁1▷ shows the outline of a curved object e.g. a vase which has been drawn on a **microcomputer**. The machine can give you a 3D picture of the shape, ◁2▷. It does this by making a model of the shape based on a series of triangles. This system of triangles is stored in the memory of the microcomputer to make up a complete model of the form of your design. If you ask the computer to give a different view, it will calculate and plot the new positions of each triangle in turn until the picture is complete ◁3▷. ◁4▷ shows how the micro can add shading to the object by giving a different tone to each of the triangles. In this way you can use the computer to view your design from any different angle and in different lights, without using anything except a computer!

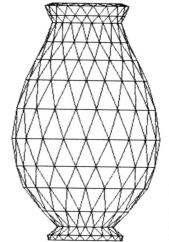

◁1▷ The outline of this curved vase was drawn on a microcomputer.

◁2▷ The microcomputer stores the details of the vase as a large number of flat triangles. This simplifies the form of the vase.

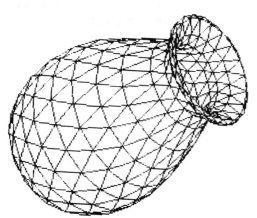

◁3▷ By calculating the position of each triangle in turn, the computer can predict what the vase will look like from different angles and show these views on screen.

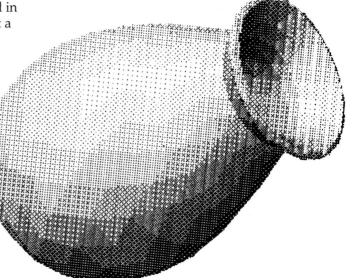

◁4▷ Shading can be added to the triangles to improve the impression of form and to give an idea of how the vase will look. Look at the varieties of shading used.

Problem solving by computer

When designing a building you need to consider all sorts of physical factors alongside the overall look of the building, e.g. heat loss, sunlight. You can use a computer to help you consider these factors by programming it with information about e.g. the heat loss through different building materials. You can then use this stored information to either calculate the heat loss of a building design by specifying the materials to be used, size etc. or use the computer to offer different solutions as to how a certain acceptable heat loss level could be achieved in your design (see ◁5▷).

In a similar way you could input information about changes in the movement of the Sun. Given the compass angle of the intended site of your house the computer could show the best position for the windows to gain the most light.

◁5▷ *A simple computer drawing of a house. The proportion of window to wall area could be calculated and adjusted on the computer to minimise heat loss and maximise sunlight.*

Simulations

As you can see modelling on a computer is extremely useful for testing all sorts of factors in relation to your design without having to construct anything! You can use a computer model to test or **simulate** something which could not easily be set up at all, like the breaking points of a bridge beam under stress ◁6▷ or predicting how the shape of a car might alter on impact (see Section 1.2). The cam test rig in 6.5 ◁5▷ could have been simulated on an animation program on your school computer.

Clearly this is only one aspect of modelling and a computer will not give you the visual quality of a block or presentation model.

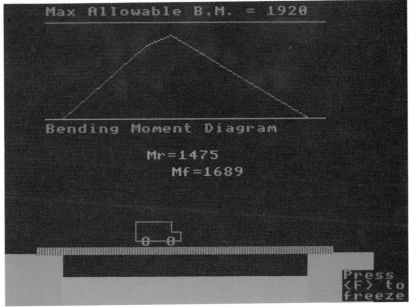

◁6▷ *A simple simulation program can show how a bridge will behave when it is loaded with vehicles of different weights.*

1 Which of the questions in this section could you investigate in the same way without using a computer? Explain why computers would be essential for the others.

2 If you were designing a computer model to work out heat loss from a school classroom, which things would you vary on the computer and which would you keep the same. For example, you might not want to vary the *size* of a door but you might want to alter the *number* of doors. You might vary the number of radiators or you might fix the number and vary the sizes. Make a list of all the items you can think of which could be variables or could be fixed. Give reasons for your decisions. Remember that your choices will be based on cost and efficiency in relation to the final building. It is much cheaper and easier to use standard size building materials.

Exercises on chapter 6

1 You have to make a model of a personal stereo as part of a GCSE project. Make a list of the materials that you would use. Explain as clearly as you can how you would construct the model and how you would finish it so that it looks realistic.

2 Several types of model have been mentioned in this book. Look at sections 1.1 and 1.2 to see how different models are used at different stages in the car industry. Explain in your own words why you think that they use a particular type of model at each stage in the design process.

3 A manufacturer of model toy cars wants a new range of display stands. The stands are to be made from card and are to be delivered to the shops flat ready for the shop keeper to assemble. There are two limits to the design: (a) the advertising material is printed on one side of the card only, (b) the car must not roll off the display. Make a full size model of such a display stand.

4 The tables in sections 6.2 and 6.3 ◁**6**▷ give you information on bonding and adhesives. Find as many trade names as you can for the different types of glue mentioned. For example a trade name for 'epoxy' is *araldite*, a trade name for PVA is *Resin W*. Make a list of this information. You could put it in table form. You will find it useful in future when you have to buy the correct glue.

5 Your teacher has been given money by the headteacher to re-equip the drawing office so that it will have model making facilities. Make two lists of the tools that she will buy, one of tools which each student should have as part of a kit, the other of tools that may be required for general use.

Glossary

Airbrush A small spray gun used for high quality artwork
Annotations Written notes which are added to a drawing to explain it

Bar chart A chart which uses bars (columns) to show how one quantity varies with another
Block diagram A chart which shows in three dimensions how one quantity varies with another
Block model A model shaped from a solid block of material
Brief The initial instructions given to a designer

Colour rendering Adding colour to a drawing to draw attention to it or improve its appearance
Computer modelling Testing or trying out an idea on a computer before manufacture
Concept drawing An artist's impression which shows the initial design idea
Constraint A restriction placed on the designer
Cut and paste A way of joining pieces of artwork or text to make a new picture or to arrange them on a page
Cut-away drawing A drawing of an object with the front surface removed to show the inside

Data graphics Ways of showing information (data) by means of pictures
Design brief See **Brief**
Design resources Any means of gathering information which will help solve a design problem
Design studio A designer's workroom

Evaluation A designer's judgement of how effective a design idea is
Exploded view A drawing in which parts of an object are spaced out to show more detail

Fixing Spraying a protective coating onto a drawing so that chalks, pastels etc do not smudge

Flow chart A way of showing the stages involved in a task and the order in which they are carried out

Flow diagram A diagram in which the width of roads or routes is varied to show how much they are used
Formal drawing An accurate drawing made with drawing instruments
Freehand drawing A drawing done by hand without using instruments

Ghosting The technique of practising a line very faintly before drawing it in
Gouache An opaque water-coloured paint
Grid A network of crossed lines used as a way of increasing accuracy in drawing
Guide box A box used to help draw pictorial views at the right angle. Several guide boxes joined together form a grid

Hatch shading A way of showing form using a series of fine lines
Highlight A bright area where light is reflected from the edge or corner of an object
Horizon A line drawn in perspective views to represent the boundary of the sky with the land

Impact graphics Images drawn to produce an immediate effect, such as for advertising or for warnings
Isometric projection A method of drawing in which all lines except verticals are drawn at 30° to the horizontal

Logo A symbol used to represent and identify a particular company or product

Marker A broad-nibbed felt pen used for adding colour to drawings
Masking Covering areas of a drawing to protect them from a colouring medium
Masking film A plastic film used for covering areas of the paper to protect them from colouring

Oblique projection A method of drawing in which the front surface is drawn flat on and the lines leading back from it are drawn at 45° to the horizontal

Pastel A crayon made of dry pigment paste
Perspective drawing A method of drawing which looks natural and gives the illusion of depth
Perspective grid A construction which helps in getting the proportions right when drawing perspective views
Pictogram A stylised image of a person, object or event
Pie chart A circular chart which shows something as a percentage of a whole. The complete circle represents 100%
Planometric projection A method of drawing based on an accurate plan turned through an angle. All verticals are shown as vertical lines, and all lines are drawn to scale
Polar graph A graph which radiates out from the pole (centre)
Presentation drawing A good quality pictorial drawing which shows a design accurately
Presentation model An accurate model of a design which gives a realistic impression of the finished product
Process drawings A sequence of drawings which show an event
Prototype An accurate model which does the job of the final design

Sketch model A model used to work out ideas
Surface development The shape of a piece of material from which a three-dimensional object can be formed

Thick and thin lines A drawing technique which makes objects look more three-dimensional

Vanishing points The points on the horizon of a perspective drawing where lines converge

Index

◆ Abbreviations 25
Airbrush 47
Annotation 26

◆ Backgrounds 41, 44, 45
Bar charts 67
Bisecting a line 54
Bisecting an angle 54
Block diagrams 67
Block models 76
Briefs 2

◆ Carb-Othello 45
Colour 32
Colour coding 38
Colour rendering 8
Colouring techniques 40, 42
Compass angles 54
Computer modelling 3, 4, 86
Computer simulations 87
Concept drawings 2
Constraints 10, 12
Construction kits 82
Crayons 40
Cut and paste 8, 50
Cut-away drawings 5, 33, 39
Cutting circles 55

◆ 3D 3
Data graphics 66
Database 3
Design 2
Design briefs 2, 10
Design ideas 2
Design resources 6
Design studios 6
Detail drawings 27
Digitizing 3, 51
Dimensions 19, 24
Directional symbols 64
Dividing a line 28, 54
Dividing an angle 54
Drawings, concept 2
cut-away 5

◆ Elevations 20
Equipment 8
Evaluation 7, 13, 14
Exploded views 32, 34, 35

◆ First angle orthographic
projection 21, 24
Fixing 8
Flow charts 70
Flow diagrams 69
Folder resources 7
Form 17
Formal drawing 21
Freehand drawing 16

◆ Geometrical solids 58
Geometry 54
Ghosting 16, 28
Gouache 41
Grids 30
Guide boxes 17, 31

◆ Hatch shading 40
Hexagons 57
Hidden detail 25, 32
Highlights 41
Horizon 18

◆ Impact graphics 64
Initial ideas 2, 10, 12
Instruction sheets 34
Isometric curves 29
Isometric projection 27, 29

◆ Letrajet 46
Lines 24
Logos 65

◆ Markers 41
Masking 42, 46
Masking film 42
Materials, designing 8
modelling 77
Modelling 3, 78
computer 3
materials for 79
mathematical 4
part 80
presentation 3, 13, 84
prototype 85
sheet 78
sketch 80
Modelling tools 74

◆ Natural lines 16, 32
Nuts and bolts 25

◆ Oblique curves 29
Oblique projection 27
Octagons 57
Organization charts 70
Orthographic projection 20, 24, 26,
30, 33
Orthographic sketching 26

◆ Parallel pictorial projections 27
Pastel rendering 43
Pastels 45
Perspective drawing 18, 20, 30
Perspective grids 31
Photocopiers 50
Photographs 26, 51
Pictograms 64
Pictorial charts 69
Pictorial views 28
Pie charts 66
Planometric projection 23
Polar graphs 68
Polygons, universal
constructions 57
Presentation drawing 5, 10
Presentation models 13, 84
Prisms 17
Process drawings 71
Proportions 17, 19, 23
Prototypes 7

◆ Reflection lines 48
Regular polygons 56
Rendering colour 8
Resource folders 7

◆ Sections 20, 25, 33
See-through drawings 33, 34
Sequential drawings 34
Shade 40
Shading, hatch 40
Shadows 41, 60
Single-point perspective 22
Sketch models 7
Sketch orthographic projection 26
Sketching 8, 16
Slide projectors 50
Spatter spray 46
Sprays 46
Surface development 58

◆ Tangents 55
Test rigs 83
Texture 40, 48
Thick and thin lines 17
Third angle orthographic
projection 21, 24
Touching circles 55
Two point perspective 18, 20, 30

◆ Vanishing points 18
Video images 51
Visual clues 48

◆ Wire-frame diagrams 4, 86
Word processing 50

◆ x-y graphs 66